Instant Vortex Dual Zone Air Fryer Cookbook 2024

1900 Day Easy, Crispy and Flavorful Instant Vortex Dual Zone Air Fryer Recipes to Cook Faster and Healthier

Anne N. Fitzwater

All Rights Reserved.

The content contained within this book may not be reproduced, duplicated, or transmitted without direct written permission from the author or the publisher. Under no circumstances will any blame or legal responsibility be held against the publisher, or author, for any damages, reparation, or monetary loss due to the information contained within this book, either directly or indirectly.

Legal Notice: This book is copyright protected. It is only for personal use. You cannot amend, distribute, sell, use, quote or paraphrase any part, or the content within this book, without the consent of the author or publisher.

Disclaimer Notice:

Please note the information contained within this document is for educational and entertainment purposes only. All effort has been executed to present accurate, up to date, reliable, complete information. No warranties of any kind are declared or implied. Readers acknowledge that the author is not engaged in the rendering of legal, financial, medical, or professional advice. The content within this book has been derived from various sources. Please consult a licensed professional before attempting any techniques outlined in this book. By reading this document, the reader agrees that under no circumstances is the author responsible for any losses, direct or indirect, that are incurred as a result of the use of the information contained within this document, including, but not limited to, errors, omissions, or inaccuracies.

CONTENTS

MEASUREMENT CONVERSIONS 12

Breakfast Recipes 14

Red Pepper And Feta Frittata And Bacon Eggs On The Go 14

Simple Bagels 14

Asparagus And Bell Pepper Strata And Greek Bagels 15

Air Fried Bacon And Eggs 15

Bacon Cheese Egg With Avocado And Potato Nuggets 16

Mushroom-and-tomato Stuffed Hash Browns 16

Potatoes Lyonnaise 17

Sausage & Bacon Omelet 17

Bagels 17

Sweet Potato Sausage Hash 18

Onion Omelette And Buffalo Egg Cups 18

Wholemeal Blueberry Muffins 19

Vanilla Strawberry Doughnuts 19

Turkey Ham Muffins 19

Bacon-and-eggs Avocado And Simple Scotch Eggs 20

Egg White Muffins 20

Spinach Omelet And Bacon, Egg, And Cheese Roll Ups 21

Jalapeño Popper Egg Cups And Cheddar Soufflés 21

Red Pepper And Feta Frittata 22

Bacon, Cheese, And Avocado Melt & Cheesy Scrambled Eggs 22

Egg And Bacon Muffins 22

Salmon Quiche 23

Cheesy Scrambled Eggs And Egg And Bacon Muffins 23

Buttermilk Biscuits With Roasted Stone Fruit Compote 24

Baked Peach Oatmeal 24

Buffalo Chicken Breakfast Muffins 25

Sesame Bagels 25

Sausage With Eggs 25

Breakfast Sausage And Cauliflower 26

Breakfast Potatoes 26

Perfect Cinnamon Toast 26

Cajun Breakfast Sausage 27

Nutty Granola 27

Sausage And Egg Breakfast Burrito 27

Parmesan Sausage Egg Muffins 28

Tomato And Mozzarella Bruschetta And Portobello Eggs Benedict 28

Air Fried Sausage 28

Eggs In Avocado Cups 29

Cheddar-ham-corn Muffins 29

Canadian Bacon Muffin Sandwiches And All-in-one Toast 29

Vegetables And Sides Recipes 30

Fried Avocado Tacos 30

Zucchini With Stuffing 30

Rosemary Asparagus & Potatoes 31

Kale And Spinach Chips 31

Buffalo Bites 31

Fried Asparagus 32

Acorn Squash Slices 32

Stuffed Sweet Potatoes 32

Green Salad With Crispy Fried Goat Cheese And Baked Croutons 33

GGarlic-rosemary Brussels Sprouts 33

arlic-herb Fried Squash 34

Fried Artichoke Hearts 34

Balsamic Vegetables 34

Caprese Panini With Zucchini Chips 35

Bacon Wrapped Corn Cob 35

Buffalo Seitan With Crispy Zucchini Noodles 36

Potatoes & Beans 36

Potato And Parsnip Latkes With Baked Apples 37

Green Beans With Baked Potatoes 37

Falafel 38

Fish And Seafood Recipes 38

Buttered Mahi-mahi 38

Chili Honey Salmon 39

Tuna Patties With Spicy Sriracha Sauce Coconut Prawns 39

Tender Juicy Honey Glazed Salmon 39

Lemon Butter Salmon 40

Tandoori Prawns 40

Pretzel-crusted Catfish 40

Fish And Chips 41

"fried" Fish With Seasoned Potato Wedges 41

Italian Baked Cod 42

Cod With Jalapeño 42

Chili Lime Tilapia 42

Marinated Ginger Garlic Salmon 42

Bang Bang Shrimp With Roasted Bok Choy 43

Cajun Scallops 43

Fish Tacos 44

Tilapia Sandwiches With Tartar Sauce 44

Steamed Cod With Garlic And Swiss Chard 45

Parmesan Mackerel With Coriander And Garlic Butter Prawns Scampi 45

Flavorful Salmon Fillets 45

Prawn Dejonghe Skewers 46

Scallops 46

Fried Prawns 46

Garlic Shrimp With Pasta Alfredo 47

Fried Lobster Tails 47

Classic Fish Sticks With Tartar Sauce 48

Tuna Patties 48

Two-way Salmon 49

Lemon-pepper Trout 49

Garlic Butter Prawns Scampi & Coconut Prawns 49

Smoked Salmon 50

Basil Cheese S·saltalmon 50

Cajun Catfish Cakes With Cheese 50

Parmesan Fish Fillets 51

Scallops And Spinach With Cream Sauce And Confetti Salmon Burgers 51

Snapper Scampi 52

Roasted Salmon Fillets & Chilli Lime Prawns 52

Furikake Salmon 52

Tuna With Herbs 53

Herb Lemon Mussels 53

Codfish With Herb Vinaigrette 53

Poultry Recipes **54**

Buttermilk Fried Chicken	54
Crispy Sesame Chicken	54
Buffalo Chicken	55
Cornish Hen With Baked Potatoes	55
Simply Terrific Turkey Meatballs	55
Fajita Chicken Strips & Barbecued Chicken With Creamy Coleslaw	56
Cheddar-stuffed Chicken	56
Lemon Chicken Thighs	57
Curried Orange Honey Chicken	57
Chicken & Veggies	57
Teriyaki Chicken Skewers	58
Bbq Cheddar-stuffed Chicken Breasts	58
Juicy Duck Breast	58
Chicken With Pineapple And Peach	59
Crusted Chicken Breast	59
Jerk Chicken Thighs	59
Chicken Leg Piece	60
Ranch Turkey Tenders With Roasted Vegetable Salad	60
Chicken And Vegetable Fajitas	61
Goat Cheese–stuffed Chicken Breast With Broiled Zucchini And Cherry Tomatoes	61
Crispy Fried Quail	62
Yummy Chicken Breasts	62
Honey-glazed Chicken Thighs	62
Air Fried Chicken Potatoes With Sun-dried Tomato	63
Chicken And Broccoli	63
Bacon-wrapped Chicken	64
Roasted Garlic Chicken Pizza With Cauliflower "wings"	64

Glazed Thighs With French Fries 65

Bell Pepper Stuffed Chicken Roll-ups 65

Balsamic Duck Breast 65

Cornish Hen With Asparagus 66

Chicken Caprese 66

Chicken Legs With Leeks 66

Wild Rice And Kale Stuffed Chicken Thighs 67

Chipotle Drumsticks 67

Chicken And Potatoes 67

Thai Chicken With Cucumber And Chili Salad 68

Spicy Chicken 68

Spicy Chicken Sandwiches With "fried" Pickles 69

Hawaiian Chicken Bites 69

Beef, Pork, And Lamb Recipes 70

Sausage Meatballs 70

Bacon-wrapped Filet Mignon 70

Minute Steak Roll-ups 70

Tasty Lamb Patties 71

Goat Cheese-stuffed Bavette Steak 71

Bbq Pork Spare Ribs 71

Sausage-stuffed Peppers 72

Air Fried Lamb Chops 72

Sumptuous Pizza Tortilla Rolls 72

Simple Beef Sirloin Roast 73

Curry-crusted Lamb Chops With Baked Brown Sugar Acorn Squash 73

Mustard Pork Chops 73

Steak And Asparagus Bundles 74

Pigs In A Blanket With Spinach-artichoke Stuffed Mushrooms 74

Mojito Lamb Chops 75

Beef And Bean Taquitos With Mexican Rice 75

Hot Dogs Wrapped In Bacon 76

Garlic Butter Steaks 76

Air Fryer Meatloaves 76

Honey-baked Pork Loin 77

Stuffed Beef Fillet With Feta Cheese 77

Blue Cheese Steak Salad 77

Gochujang Brisket 78

Simple Strip Steak 78

Roasted Beef 78

Mustard Rubbed Lamb Chops 79

Garlic-rosemary Pork Loin With Scalloped Potatoes And Cauliflower 79

Cilantro Lime Steak 80

Bacon Wrapped Pork Tenderloin 80

Asian Pork Skewers 80

Easy Breaded Pork Chops 81

Snacks And Appetizers Recipes 81

Beef Skewers 81

Garlic Bread 81

Cheese Drops 82

Chicken Tenders 82

Kale Chips 82

Five-ingredient Falafel With Garlic-yoghurt Sauce 83

Buffalo Wings Honey-garlic Wings 83

Fried Pickles 84

Roasted Tomato Bruschetta With Toasty Garlic Bread 84

Mexican Jalapeno Poppers 84

Crunchy Basil White Beans And Artichoke And Olive Pitta Flatbread 85

Healthy Spinach Balls 85

Sausage Balls With Cheese 85

Fried Okra 86

Dijon Cheese Sandwich 86

Crab Cake Poppers 86

Bacon-wrapped Shrimp And Jalapeño 87

Veggie Shrimp Toast 87

Cheese Corn Fritters 87

Stuffed Bell Peppers 87

Desserts Recipes 88

Brownies Muffins 88

Monkey Bread 88

Baked Brazilian Pineapple 88

Butter Cake 89

Caramelized Fruit Skewers 89

Butter And Chocolate Chip Cookies 89

Almond Shortbread 90

Oreo Rolls 90

Pumpkin Muffins With Cinnamon 90

Honeyed, Roasted Apples With Walnuts & Rhubarb And Strawberry Crumble 91

Baked Apples 91

Fruity Blackberry Crisp 91

Fried Dough With Roasted Strawberries 92

Dehydrated Peaches 92

Fried Oreos 92

Banana Spring Rolls With Hot Fudge Dip 93

Simple Cheesecake 93

Biscuit Doughnuts 94

Moist Chocolate Espresso Muffins 94

Blueberry Pie Egg Rolls 94

Homemade Mint Pie And Strawberry Pecan Pie 95

Lime Bars 95

Air Fryer Sweet Twists 95

Walnuts Fritters 96

Maple-pecan Tart With Sea Salt 96

Easy Mini Chocolate Chip Pan Cookie 97

Cake In The Air Fryer 97

Molten Chocolate Almond Cakes 97

Apple Fritters 98

Spiced Apple Cake 98

RECIPES INDEX 99

MEASUREMENT CONVERSIONS

BASIC KITCHEN CONVERSIONS & EQUIVALENTS

DRY MEASUREMENTS CONVERSION CHART

3 TEASPOONS = 1 TABLESPOON = 1/16 CUP
6 TEASPOONS = 2 TABLESPOONS = 1/8 CUP
12 TEASPOONS = 4 TABLESPOONS = 1/4 CUP
24 TEASPOONS = 8 TABLESPOONS = 1/2 CUP
36 TEASPOONS = 12 TABLESPOONS = 3/4 CUP
48 TEASPOONS = 16 TABLESPOONS = 1 CUP

METRIC TO US COOKING CONVER-SIONS

OVEN TEMPERATURES

120 °C = 250 °F
160 °C = 320 °F
180 °C = 350 °F
205 °C = 400 °F
220 °C = 425 °F

LIQUID MEASUREMENTS CONVERSION CHART

8 FLUID OUNCES = 1 CUP = 1/2 PINT = 1/4 QUART
16 FLUID OUNCES = 2 CUPS = 1 PINT = 1/2 QUART
32 FLUID OUNCES = 4 CUPS = 2 PINTS = 1 QUART
1/4 GALLON
128 FLUID OUNCES = 16 CUPS = 8 PINTS = 4 QUARTS = 1 GALLON

BAKING IN GRAMS

1 CUP FLOUR = 140 GRAMS
1 CUP SUGAR = 150 GRAMS
1 CUP POWDERED SUGAR=160 GRAMS
1 CUP HEAVY CREAM = 235 GRAMS

VOLUME

1 MILLILITER=1/5 TEASPOON
5 ML = 1 TEASPOON
15 ML = 1 TABLESPOON
240 ML = 1 CUP OR 8 FLUID OUNCES
1 LITER=34 FL. OUNCES

WEIGHT

1 GRAM = 035 OUNCES
100 GRAMS=3.5 OUNCES
500 GRAMS = 1.1 POUNDS
1 KILOGRAM=35 OUNCES

US TO METRIC COOKING CONVERSIONS

1/5 TSP = 1 ML
1 TSP=5 ML
1 TBSP = 15 ML
1 FL OUNCE = 30 ML
1 CUP=237 ML
1 PINT (2 CUPS) = 473 ML
1 QUART (4 CUPS)=.95 LITER
1GALLON (16 CUPS)=3.8LITERS
1 OZ=28 GRAMS
1 POUND = 454 GRAMS

BUTTER

1 CUP BUTTER=2 STICKS = 8 OUNCES = 230 GRAMS=8 TABLESPOONS

WHAT DOES 1 CUP EQUAL

1 CUP = 8 FLUID OUNCES
1 CUP = 16 TABLESPOONS
1 CUP = 48 TEASPOONS
1 CUP = 1/2 PINT
1 CUP = 1/4 QUART
1 CUP = 1/16 GALLON
1 CUP = 240 ML

BAKING PAN CONVERSIONS

1 CUP ALL-PURPOSE FLOUR=4.5 OZ
1 CUP ROLLED OATS = 3 OZ 1 LARGE EGG = 1.7 OZ
1 CUP BUTTER=8OZ 1 CUP MILK = 8 OZ
1 CUP HEAVY CREAM = 8.4 OZ
1 CUP GRANULATED SUGAR=7.1 OZ
1 CUP PACKED BROWN SUGAR = 7.75 OZ
1 CUP VEGETABLE OIL = 7.7 OZ
1 CUP UNSIFTED POWDERED SUGAR = 4.4 OZ

BAKING PAN CONVERSIONS

9-INCH ROUND CAKE PAN= 12 CUPS
10-INCH TUBE PAN =16 CUPS
11-INCH BUNDT PAN = 12 CUPS
9-INCH SPRINGFORM PAN = 10 CUPS
9 X 5 INCH LOAF PAN=8 CUPS
9-INCH SQUARE PAN=8 CUPS

Breakfast Recipes

Red Pepper And Feta Frittata And Bacon Eggs On The Go

Servings: 5
Cooking Time: 20 Minutes
Ingredients:
- Red Pepper and Feta Frittata:
- Olive oil cooking spray
- 8 large eggs
- 1 medium red pepper, diced
- ½ teaspoon salt
- ½ teaspoon black pepper
- 1 garlic clove, minced
- 120 ml feta, divided
- Bacon Eggs on the Go:
- 2 eggs
- 110 g bacon, cooked
- Salt and ground black pepper, to taste

Directions:
1. Make the Red Pepper and Feta Frittata :
2. Preheat the air fryer to 180ºC. Lightly coat the inside of a 6-inch round cake pan with olive oil cooking spray.
3. In a large bowl, beat the eggs for 1 to 2 minutes, or until well combined.
4. Add the red pepper, salt, black pepper, and garlic to the eggs, and mix together until the red pepper is distributed throughout.
5. Fold in 60 ml the feta cheese.
6. Pour the egg mixture into the prepared cake pan, and sprinkle the remaining 60 ml feta over the top.
7. Place into the zone 1 air fryer basket and bake for 18 to 20 minutes, or until the eggs are set in the center.
8. Remove from the air fryer and allow to cool for 5 minutes before serving.
9. Make the Bacon Eggs on the Go :
10. Preheat the air fryer to 205ºC. Put liners in a regular cupcake tin.
11. Crack an egg into each of the cups and add the bacon. Season with some pepper and salt.
12. Bake in the preheated zone 2 air fryer basket for 15 minutes, or until the eggs are set. Serve warm.

Simple Bagels

Servings: 4
Cooking Time: 12 Minutes
Ingredients:
- 125g plain flour
- 2 teaspoons baking powder
- Salt, as required
- 240g plain Greek yogurt
- 1 egg, beaten
- 1 tablespoon water
- 1 tablespoon sesame seeds
- 1 teaspoon coarse salt

Directions:
1. In a large bowl, mix together the flour, baking powder and salt.
2. Add the yogurt and mix until a dough ball forms.
3. Place the dough onto a lightly floured surface and then cut into 4 equal-sized balls.
4. Roll each ball into a 17 – 19 cm rope and then join ends to shape a bagel.
5. Grease basket of Instant 2-Basket Air Fryer.
6. Press your chosen zone - "Zone 1" or "Zone 2" and then rotate the knob to select "Air Fry".
7. Set the temperature to 165 degrees C and then set the time for 5 minutes to preheat.
8. Meanwhile, in a small bowl, add egg and water and mix well.
9. Brush the bagels with egg mixture evenly.
10. Sprinkle the top of each bagel with sesame seeds and salt, pressing lightly.
11. After preheating, arrange 2 bagels into the basket of each zone.
12. Slide the basket into the Air Fryer and set the time for 12 minutes.
13. After cooking time is completed, remove the bagels from Air Fryer and serve warm.

Asparagus And Bell Pepper Strata And Greek Bagels

Servings: 6
Cooking Time: 14 To 20 Minutes
Ingredients:
- Asparagus and Bell Pepper Strata:
- 8 large asparagus spears, trimmed and cut into 2-inch pieces
- 80 ml shredded carrot
- 120 ml chopped red pepper
- 2 slices wholemeal bread, cut into ½-inch cubes
- 3 egg whites
- 1 egg
- 3 tablespoons 1% milk
- ½ teaspoon dried thyme
- Greek Bagels:
- 120 ml self-raising flour, plus more for dusting
- 120 ml plain Greek yoghurt
- 1 egg
- 1 tablespoon water
- 4 teaspoons sesame seeds or za'atar
- Cooking oil spray
- 1 tablespoon butter, melted

Directions:
1. Make the Asparagus and Bell Pepper Strata :
2. In a baking pan, combine the asparagus, carrot, red bell pepper, and 1 tablespoon of water. Bake in the air fryer at 166°C for 3 to 5 minutes, or until crisp-tender. Drain well.
3. Add the bread cubes to the vegetables and gently toss.
4. In a medium bowl, whisk the egg whites, egg, milk, and thyme until frothy.
5. Pour the egg mixture into the pan. Bake in the zone 1 drawer for 11 to 15 minutes, or until the strata is slightly puffy and set and the top starts to brown. Serve.
6. Make the Greek Bagels :
7. In a large bowl, using a wooden spoon, stir together the flour and yoghurt until a tacky dough forms. Transfer the dough to a lightly floured work surface and roll the dough into a ball.
8. Cut the dough into 2 pieces and roll each piece into a log. Form each log into a bagel shape, pinching the ends together.
9. In a small bowl, whisk the egg and water. Brush the egg wash on the bagels.
10. Sprinkle 2 teaspoons of the toppings on each bagel and gently press it into the dough.
11. Insert the crisper plate into the zone 2 drawer and the drawer into the unit. Preheat the drawer by selecting BAKE, setting the temperature to 166°C, and setting the time to 3 minutes. Select START/STOP to begin.
12. Once the drawer is preheated, spray the crisper plate with cooking spray. Drizzle the bagels with the butter and place them into the drawer.
13. Select BAKE, set the temperature to 166°C, and set the time to 10 minutes. Select START/STOP to begin.
14. When the cooking is complete, the bagels should be lightly golden on the outside. Serve warm.

Air Fried Bacon And Eggs

Servings: 1
Cooking Time: 10 Minutes
Ingredients:
- 2 eggs
- 2 slices bacon

Directions:
1. Grease a ramekin using cooking spray.
2. Install the crisper plate in the zone 1 drawer and place the bacon inside it. Insert the drawer into the unit.
3. Crack the eggs and add them to the greased ramekin.
4. Install the crisper plate in the zone 2 drawer and place the ramekin inside it. Insert the drawer into the unit.
5. Select zone 1 to AIR FRY for 9–11 minutes at 400 degrees F/ 200 degrees C. Select zone 2 to AIR FRY for 8–9 minutes at 350 degrees F/ 175 degrees C. Press SYNC.
6. Press START/STOP to begin cooking.
7. Enjoy!

Nutrition:
- (Per serving) Calories 331 | Fat 24.5g | Sodium 1001mg | Carbs 1.2g | Fiber 0g | Sugar 0.7g | Protein 25.3g

Bacon Cheese Egg With Avocado And Potato Nuggets

Servings: 8
Cooking Time: 20 Minutes
Ingredients:
- Bacon Cheese Egg with Avocado:
- 6 large eggs
- 60 ml double cream
- 350 ml chopped cauliflower
- 235 ml shredded medium Cheddar cheese
- 1 medium avocado, peeled and pitted
- 8 tablespoons full-fat sour cream
- 2 spring onions, sliced on the bias
- 12 slices bacon, cooked and crumbled
- Potato Nuggets:
- 1 teaspoon extra virgin olive oil
- 1 clove garlic, minced
- 1 L kale, rinsed and chopped
- 475 ml potatoes, boiled and mashed
- 30 ml milk
- Salt and ground black pepper, to taste
- Cooking spray

Directions:
1. Make the Bacon Cheese Egg with Avocado :
2. In a medium bowl, whisk eggs and cream together. Pour into a round baking dish.
3. Add cauliflower and mix, then top with Cheddar. Place dish into the zone 1 air fryer drawer.
4. Adjust the temperature to 160°C and set the timer for 20 minutes.
5. When completely cooked, eggs will be firm and cheese will be browned. Slice into four pieces.
6. Slice avocado and divide evenly among pieces. Top each piece with 2 tablespoons sour cream, sliced spring onions, and crumbled bacon.
7. Make the Potato Nuggets :
8. Preheat the zone 2 air fryer drawer to 200°C.
9. In a skillet over medium heat, sauté the garlic in the olive oil, until it turns golden brown. Sauté with the kale for an additional 3 minutes and remove from the heat.
10. Mix the mashed potatoes, kale and garlic in a bowl. Pour in the milk and sprinkle with salt and pepper.
11. Shape the mixture into nuggets and spritz with cooking spray.
12. Put in the zone 2 air fryer drawer and air fry for 15 minutes, flip the nuggets halfway through cooking to make sure the nuggets fry evenly.
13. Serve immediately.

Mushroom-and-tomato Stuffed Hash Browns

Servings: 4
Cooking Time: 20 Minutes
Ingredients:
- Olive oil cooking spray
- 1 tablespoon plus 2 teaspoons olive oil, divided
- 110 g baby mushrooms, diced
- 1 spring onion, white parts and green parts, diced
- 1 garlic clove, minced
- 475 ml shredded potatoes
- ½ teaspoon salt
- ¼ teaspoon black pepper
- 1 plum tomato, diced
- 120 ml shredded mozzarella

Directions:
1. Lightly coat the inside of a 6-inch cake pan with olive oil cooking spray. In a small skillet, heat 2 teaspoons olive oil over medium heat. Add the mushrooms, spring onion, and garlic, and cook for 4 to 5 minutes, or until they have softened and are beginning to show some color.
2. Remove from heat. Meanwhile, in a large bowl, combine the potatoes, salt, pepper, and the remaining tablespoon olive oil. Toss until all potatoes are well coated. Pour half of the potatoes into the bottom of the cake pan.
3. Top with the mushroom mixture, tomato, and mozzarella. Spread the remaining potatoes over the top. Place the cake pan into the zone 1 drawer.
4. Select Bake button and adjust temperature to 190°C, set time to 12 to 15 minutes and press Start. Until the top is golden brown, remove from the air fryer and allow to cool for 5 minutes before slicing and serving.

Potatoes Lyonnaise

Servings: 4
Cooking Time: 31 Minutes
Ingredients:
- 1 sweet/mild onion, sliced
- 1 teaspoon butter, melted
- 1 teaspoon brown sugar
- 2 large white potatoes (about 450 g in total), sliced ½-inch thick
- 1 tablespoon vegetable oil
- Salt and freshly ground black pepper, to taste

Directions:
1. Preheat the air fryer to 188°C.
2. Toss the sliced onions, melted butter and brown sugar together in the zone 1 air fryer drawer. Air fry for 8 minutes, shaking the drawer occasionally to help the onions cook evenly.
3. While the onions are cooking, bring a saucepan of salted water to a boil on the stovetop. Par-cook the potatoes in boiling water for 3 minutes. Drain the potatoes and pat them dry with a clean kitchen towel.
4. Add the potatoes to the onions in the zone 1 air fryer drawer and drizzle with vegetable oil. Toss to coat the potatoes with the oil and season with salt and freshly ground black pepper.
5. Increase the air fryer temperature to 204°C and air fry for 20 minutes, tossing the vegetables a few times during the cooking time to help the potatoes brown evenly.
6. Season with salt and freshly ground black pepper and serve warm.

Sausage & Bacon Omelet

Servings: 4
Cooking Time: 10 Minutes
Ingredients:
- 8 eggs
- 2 bacon slices, chopped
- 4 sausages, chopped
- 2 yellow onions, chopped

Directions:
1. In a bowl, crack the eggs and beat well.
2. Add the remaining ingredients and gently stir to combine.
3. Divide the mixture into 2 small baking pans.
4. Press your chosen zone - "Zone 1" or "Zone 2" and then rotate the knob to select "Air Fry".
5. Set the temperature to 160 degrees C and then set the time for 5 minutes to preheat.
6. After preheating, arrange 1 pan into the basket of each zone.
7. Slide the basket into the Air Fryer and set the time for 10 minutes.
8. After cooking time is completed, remove the both pans from Air Fryer.
9. Cut each omelet in wedges and serve hot.

Bagels

Servings: 8
Cooking Time: 15 Minutes
Ingredients:
- 2 cups self-rising flour
- 2 cups non-fat plain Greek yogurt
- 2 beaten eggs for egg wash (optional)
- ½ cup sesame seeds (optional)

Directions:
1. In a medium mixing bowl, combine the self-rising flour and Greek yogurt using a wooden spoon.
2. Knead the dough for about 5 minutes on a lightly floured board.
3. Divide the dough into four equal pieces and roll each into a thin rope, securing the ends to form a bagel shape.
4. Install a crisper plate in both drawers. Place 4 bagels in a single layer in each drawer. Insert the drawers into the unit.
5. Select zone 1, select AIR FRY, set temperature to 360 degrees F/ 180 degrees C, and set time to 15 minutes. Select MATCH to match zone 2 settings to zone 1. Select START/STOP to begin.
6. Once the timer has finished, remove the bagels from the units.
7. Serve and enjoy!

Nutrition:
- (Per serving) Calories 202 | Fat 4.5g | Sodium 55mg | Carbs 31.3g | Fiber 2.7g | Sugar 4.7g | Protein 8.7g

Sweet Potato Sausage Hash

Servings: 4
Cooking Time: 20 Minutes
Ingredients:
- 1½ pounds sweet potato, peeled and diced into ½-inch pieces
- 1 tablespoon minced garlic
- 1 teaspoon kosher salt plus more, as desired
- Ground black pepper, as desired
- 2 tablespoons canola oil
- 1 tablespoon dried sage
- 1-pound uncooked mild ground breakfast sausage
- ½ large onion, peeled and diced
- ½ teaspoon ground cinnamon
- 1 teaspoon chili powder
- 4 large eggs, poached or fried (optional)

Directions:
1. Toss the sweet potatoes with the garlic, salt, pepper, and canola oil in a mixing bowl.
2. Install the crisper plate in the zone 1 drawer, fill it with the sweet potato mixture, and insert the drawer in the unit.
3. Place the ground sausage in the zone 2 drawer (without the crisper plate) and place it in the unit.
4. Select zone 1, then AIR FRY, and set the temperature to 400 degrees F/ 200 degrees C with a 30-minute timer.
5. Select zone 2, then ROAST, then set the temperature to 400 degrees F/ 200 degrees C with a 20-minute timer. SYNC is the option to choose. To begin cooking, press the START/STOP button.
6. When the zone 1 and zone 2 times have reached 10 minutes, press START/STOP and remove the drawers from the unit. Shake each for 10 seconds.
7. Half of the sage should be added to the zone 1 drawer.
8. Add the onion to the zone 2 drawer and mix to incorporate. To continue cooking, press START/STOP and reinsert the drawers.
9. Remove both drawers from the unit once the cooking is finished and add the potatoes to the sausage mixture. Mix in the cinnamon, sage, chili powder, and salt until thoroughly combined.
10. When the hash is done, stir it and serve it right away with a poached or fried egg on top, if desired.

Nutrition:
- (Per serving) Calories 491 | Fat 19.5g | Sodium 736mg | Carbs 51g | Fiber 8g | Sugar 2g | Protein 26.3

Onion Omelette And Buffalo Egg Cups

Servings: 4
Cooking Time: 15 Minutes
Ingredients:
- Onion Omelette:
- 3 eggs
- Salt and ground black pepper, to taste
- ½ teaspoons soy sauce
- 1 large onion, chopped
- 2 tablespoons grated Cheddar cheese
- Cooking spray
- Buffalo Egg Cups:
- 4 large eggs
- 60 g full-fat cream cheese
- 2 tablespoons buffalo sauce
- 120 ml shredded sharp Cheddar cheese

Directions:
1. Make the Onion Omelette :
2. Preheat the zone 1 air fryer drawer to 180°C.
3. In a bowl, whisk together the eggs, salt, pepper, and soy sauce.
4. Spritz a small pan with cooking spray. Spread the chopped onion across the bottom of the pan, then transfer the pan to the zone 1 air fryer drawer.
5. Bake in the preheated air fryer for 6 minutes or until the onion is translucent.
6. Add the egg mixture on top of the onions to coat well. Add the cheese on top, then continue baking for another 6 minutes.
7. Allow to cool before serving.
8. Make the Buffalo Egg Cups :
9. Crack eggs into two ramekins.
10. In a small microwave-safe bowl, mix cream cheese, buffalo sauce, and Cheddar. Microwave for 20 seconds and then stir. Place a spoonful into each ramekin on top of the eggs.
11. Place ramekins into the zone 2 air fryer drawer.
12. Adjust the temperature to 160°C and bake for 15 minutes.
13. Serve warm.

Wholemeal Blueberry Muffins

Servings: 6
Cooking Time: 15 Minutes
Ingredients:
- Olive oil cooking spray
- 120 ml unsweetened applesauce
- 60 ml honey
- 120 ml non-fat plain Greek yoghurt
- 1 teaspoon vanilla extract
- 1 large egg
- 350 ml plus 1 tablespoon wholemeal, divided
- ½ teaspoon baking soda
- ½ teaspoon baking powder
- ½ teaspoon salt
- 120 ml blueberries, fresh or frozen

Directions:
1. Lightly coat the inside of six silicone muffin cups or a six-cup muffin tin with olive oil cooking spray.
2. In a large bowl, combine the applesauce, honey, yoghurt, vanilla, and egg and mix until smooth. Sift in 350 ml of the flour, the baking soda, baking powder, and salt into the wet mixture, then stir until just combined. In a small bowl, toss the blueberries with the remaining 1 tablespoon flour, then fold the mixture into the muffin batter.
3. Divide the mixture evenly among the prepared muffin cups and place into the zone 1 drawer of the air fryer. Bake at 182°C for 12 to 15 minutes, or until golden brown on top and a toothpick inserted into the middle of one of the muffins comes out clean. Allow to cool for 5 minutes before serving.

Vanilla Strawberry Doughnuts

Servings: 8
Cooking Time: 15 Minutes
Ingredients:
- 1 egg
- ½ cup strawberries, diced
- 80ml cup milk
- 1 tsp cinnamon
- 1 tsp baking soda
- 136g all-purpose flour
- 2 tsp vanilla
- 2 tbsp butter, melted
- 73g sugar
- ½ tsp salt

Directions:
1. In a bowl, mix flour, cinnamon, baking soda, sugar, and salt.
2. In a separate bowl, whisk egg, milk, butter, and vanilla.
3. Pour egg mixture into the flour mixture and mix until well combined.
4. Add strawberries and mix well.
5. Pour batter into the silicone doughnut moulds.
6. Insert a crisper plate in the Instant air fryer baskets.
7. Place doughnut moulds in both baskets.
8. Select zone 1, then select "air fry" mode and set the temperature to 320 degrees F for 15 minutes. Press "match" to match zone 2 settings to zone 1. Press "start/stop" to begin.

Nutrition:
- (Per serving) Calories 133 | Fat 3.8g |Sodium 339mg | Carbs 21.9g | Fiber 0.8g | Sugar 9.5g | Protein 2.7g

Turkey Ham Muffins

Servings: 16
Cooking Time: 10 Minutes
Ingredients:
- 1 egg
- 340g all-purpose flour
- 85g turkey ham, chopped
- 2 tbsp mix herbs, chopped
- 235g cheddar cheese, shredded
- 1 onion, chopped
- 2 tsp baking powder
- 2 tbsp butter, melted
- 237ml milk
- Pepper
- Salt

Directions:
1. In a large bowl, mix flour and baking powder.
2. Add egg, butter, and milk and mix until well combined.
3. Add herbs, cheese, onion, and turkey ham and mix well.
4. Insert a crisper plate in the Instant air fryer baskets.
5. Pour the batter into the silicone muffin moulds.
6. Place muffin moulds in both baskets.
7. Select zone 1, then select "air fry" mode and set the temperature to 355 degrees F for 10 minutes. Press "match" to match zone 2 settings to zone 1. Press "start/stop" to begin.

Nutrition:
- (Per serving) Calories 140 | Fat 4.8g |Sodium 126mg | Carbs 18.2g | Fiber 0.7g | Sugar 1.2g | Protein 5.8g

Bacon-and-eggs Avocado And Simple Scotch Eggs

Servings: 5
Cooking Time: 25 Minutes
Ingredients:
- Bacon-and-Eggs Avocado:
- 1 large egg
- 1 avocado, halved, peeled, and pitted
- 2 slices bacon
- Fresh parsley, for serving (optional)
- Sea salt flakes, for garnish (optional)
- Simple Scotch Eggs:
- 4 large hard boiled eggs
- 1 (340 g) package pork sausage meat
- 8 slices thick-cut bacon
- 4 wooden toothpicks, soaked in water for at least 30 minutes

Directions:
1. Make the Bacon-and-Eggs Avocado :
2. 1. Spray the zone 1 air fryer basket with avocado oil. Preheat the air fryer to 160°C. Fill a small bowl with cool water. Soft-boil the egg: Place the egg in the zone 1 air fryer basket. Air fry for 6 minutes for a soft yolk or 7 minutes for a cooked yolk. Transfer the egg to the bowl of cool water and let sit for 2 minutes. Peel and set aside. 3. Use a spoon to carve out extra space in the center of the avocado halves until the cavities are big enough to fit the soft-boiled egg. Place the soft-boiled egg in the center of one half of the avocado and replace the other half of the avocado on top, so the avocado appears whole on the outside. 4. Starting at one end of the avocado, wrap the bacon around the avocado to completely cover it. Use toothpicks to hold the bacon in place. 5. Place the bacon-wrapped avocado in the zone 1 air fryer basket and air fry for 5 minutes. Flip the avocado over and air fry for another 5 minutes, or until the bacon is cooked to your liking. Serve on a bed of fresh parsley, if desired, and sprinkle with salt flakes, if desired. 6. Best served fresh. Store extras in an airtight container in the fridge for up to 4 days. Reheat in a preheated 160°C air fryer for 4 minutes, or until heated through.
3. Make the Simple Scotch Eggs :
4. Slice the sausage meat into four parts and place each part into a large circle.
5. Put an egg into each circle and wrap it in the sausage. Put in the refrigerator for 1 hour.
6. Preheat the air fryer to 235°C.
7. Make a cross with two pieces of thick-cut bacon. Put a wrapped egg in the center, fold the bacon over top of the egg, and secure with a toothpick.
8. Air fry in the preheated zone 2 air fryer basket for 25 minutes.
9. Serve immediately.

Egg White Muffins

Servings: 8
Cooking Time: 10 Minutes
Ingredients:
- 4 slices center-cut bacon, cut into strips
- 4 ounces baby bella mushrooms, roughly chopped
- 2 ounces sun-dried tomatoes
- 2 tablespoon sliced black olives
- 2 tablespoons grated or shredded parmesan
- 2 tablespoons shredded mozzarella
- ¼ teaspoon black pepper
- ¾ cup liquid egg whites
- 2 tablespoons liquid egg whites

Directions:
1. Heat a saucepan with a little oil, add the bacon and mushrooms and cook until fully cooked and crispy, about 6–8 minutes.
2. While the bacon and mushrooms cook, mix the ¾ cup liquid egg whites, sun-dried tomato, olives, parmesan, mozzarella, and black pepper together in a large bowl.
3. Add the cooked bacon and mushrooms to the tomato and olive mixture, stirring everything together.
4. Spoon the mixture into muffin molds, followed by 2 tablespoons of egg whites over the top.
5. Place half the muffins mold in zone 1 and half in zone 2, then insert the drawers into the unit.
6. Select zone 1, select AIR FRY, set temperature to 390 degrees F/ 200 degrees C, and set time to 22 minutes.
7. Select MATCH to match zone 2 settings to zone 1. Press the START/STOP button to begin cooking.
8. When cooking is complete, remove the molds and enjoy!

Nutrition:
- (Per serving) Calories 104 | Fat 5.6g | Sodium 269mg | Carbs 3.5g | Fiber 0.8g | Sugar 0.3g | Protein 10.3g

Spinach Omelet And Bacon, Egg, And Cheese Roll Ups

Servings: 6
Cooking Time: 15 Minutes
Ingredients:
- Spinach Omelet:
- 4 large eggs
- 350 ml chopped fresh spinach leaves
- 2 tablespoons peeled and chopped brown onion
- 2 tablespoons salted butter, melted
- 120 ml shredded mild Cheddar cheese
- ¼ teaspoon salt
- Bacon, Egg, and Cheese Roll Ups:
- 2 tablespoons unsalted butter
- 60 ml chopped onion
- ½ medium green pepper, seeded and chopped
- 6 large eggs
- 12 slices bacon
- 235 ml shredded sharp Cheddar cheese
- 120 ml mild salsa, for dipping

Directions:
1. Make the Spinach Omelet :
2. In an ungreased round nonstick baking dish, whisk eggs. Stir in spinach, onion, butter, Cheddar, and salt.
3. Place dish into zone 1 air fryer basket. Adjust the temperature to 160°C and bake for 12 minutes. Omelet will be done when browned on the top and firm in the middle.
4. Slice in half and serve warm on two medium plates.
5. Make the Bacon, Egg, and Cheese Roll Ups :
6. In a medium skillet over medium heat, melt butter. Add onion and pepper to the skillet and sauté until fragrant and onions are translucent, about 3 minutes.
7. Whisk eggs in a small bowl and pour into skillet. Scramble eggs with onions and peppers until fluffy and fully cooked, about 5 minutes. Remove from heat and set aside.
8. On work surface, place three slices of bacon side by side, overlapping about ¼ inch. Place 60 ml scrambled eggs in a heap on the side closest to you and sprinkle 60 ml cheese on top of the eggs.
9. Tightly roll the bacon around the eggs and secure the seam with a toothpick if necessary. Place each roll into the zone 2 air fryer basket.
10. Adjust the temperature to 175°C and air fry for 15 minutes. Rotate the rolls halfway through the cooking time.
11. Bacon will be brown and crispy when completely cooked. Serve immediately with salsa for dipping.

Jalapeño Popper Egg Cups And Cheddar Soufflés

Servings: 6
Cooking Time: 12 Minutes
Ingredients:
- Jalapeño Popper Egg Cups:
- 4 large eggs
- 60 ml chopped pickled jalapeños
- 60 g full-fat cream cheese
- 120 ml shredded sharp Cheddar cheese
- Cheddar Soufflés:
- 3 large eggs, whites and yolks separated
- ¼ teaspoon cream of tartar
- 120 ml shredded sharp Cheddar cheese
- 85 g cream cheese, softened

Directions:
1. Make the Jalapeño Popper Egg Cups :
2. In a medium bowl, beat the eggs, then pour into four silicone muffin cups.
3. In a large microwave-safe bowl, place jalapeños, cream cheese, and Cheddar. Microwave for 30 seconds and stir. Take a spoonful, approximately ¼ of the mixture, and place it in the center of one of the egg cups. Repeat with remaining mixture.
4. Place egg cups into the zone 1 air fryer drawer.
5. Adjust the temperature to 160°C and bake for 10 minutes.
6. Serve warm.
7. Make the Cheddar Soufflés :
8. In a large bowl, beat egg whites together with cream of tartar until soft peaks form, about 2 minutes.
9. In a separate medium bowl, beat egg yolks, Cheddar, and cream cheese together until frothy, about 1 minute. Add egg yolk mixture to whites, gently folding until combined.
10. Pour mixture evenly into four ramekins greased with cooking spray. Place ramekins into the zone 2 air fryer drawer. Adjust the temperature to 176°C and bake for 12 minutes. Eggs will be browned on the top and firm in the center when done. Serve warm.

Red Pepper And Feta Frittata

Servings: 4
Cooking Time: 20 Minutes
Ingredients:
- Olive oil cooking spray
- 8 large eggs
- 1 medium red pepper, diced
- ½ teaspoon salt
- ½ teaspoon black pepper
- 1 garlic clove, minced
- 120 ml feta, divided

Directions:
1. Lightly coat the inside of a 6-inch round cake pan with olive oil cooking spray. In a large bowl, beat the eggs for 1 to 2 minutes, or until well combined.
2. Add the red pepper, salt, black pepper, and garlic to the eggs, and mix together until the red pepper is distributed throughout. Fold in 60 ml the feta cheese.
3. Pour the egg mixture into the prepared cake pan, and sprinkle the remaining 60 ml feta over the top. Place into the zone 1 drawer. Select Bake button and adjust temperature to 180°C, set time to 18 to 20 minutes and press Start.
4. Remove from the air fryer after the end and allow to cool for 5 minutes before serving.

Bacon, Cheese, And Avocado Melt & Cheesy Scrambled Eggs

Servings: 4
Cooking Time: 9 Minutes
Ingredients:
- Bacon, Cheese, and Avocado Melt:
- 1 avocado
- 4 slices cooked bacon, chopped
- 2 tablespoons salsa
- 1 tablespoon double cream
- 60 ml shredded Cheddar cheese
- Cheesy Scrambled Eggs:
- 1 teaspoon unsalted butter
- 2 large eggs
- 2 tablespoons milk
- 2 tablespoons shredded Cheddar cheese
- Salt and freshly ground black pepper, to taste

Directions:
1. Make the Bacon, Cheese, and Avocado Melt :
2. Preheat the zone 1 air fryer drawer to 204°C.
3. Slice the avocado in half lengthwise and remove the stone. To ensure the avocado halves do not roll in the drawer, slice a thin piece of skin off the base.
4. In a small bowl, combine the bacon, salsa, and cream. Divide the mixture between the avocado halves and top with the cheese.
5. Place the avocado halves in the zone 1 air fryer drawer and air fry for 3 to 5 minutes until the cheese has melted and begins to brown. Serve warm.
6. Make the Cheesy Scrambled Eggs :
7. Preheat the zone 2 air fryer drawer to 150°C. Place the butter in a baking pan and cook for 1 to 2 minutes, until melted.
8. In a small bowl, whisk together the eggs, milk, and cheese. Season with salt and black pepper. Transfer the mixture to the pan.
9. Cook for 3 minutes. Stir the eggs and push them toward the center of the pan.
10. Cook for another 2 minutes, then stir again. Cook for another 2 minutes, until the eggs are just cooked. Serve warm.

Egg And Bacon Muffins

Servings: 1
Cooking Time: 15 Minutes
Ingredients:
- 2 eggs
- Salt and ground black pepper, to taste
- 1 tablespoon green pesto
- 85 g shredded Cheddar cheese
- 140 g cooked bacon
- 1 spring onion, chopped

Directions:
1. Line a cupcake tin with parchment paper. Beat the eggs with pepper, salt, and pesto in a bowl. Mix in the cheese.
2. Pour the eggs into the cupcake tin and top with the bacon and spring onion.
3. Place the cupcake tin into the zone 1 drawer and bake at 180°C for 15 minutes, or until the egg is set. Serve immediately.

Salmon Quiche

Servings: 4
Cooking Time: 20 Minutes
Ingredients:
- 275g salmon fillets, chopped
- Salt and ground black pepper, as required
- 1 tablespoon fresh lemon juice
- 2 egg yolks
- 7 tablespoons chilled butter
- 165g flour
- 2 tablespoons cold water
- 4 eggs
- 6 tablespoons whipping cream
- 2 spring onions, chopped

Directions:
1. In a bowl, mix together the salmon, salt, black pepper and lemon juice. Set aside.
2. In another bowl, add egg yolk, butter, flour and water and mix until a dough forms.
3. Divide the dough into 2 portions.
4. Place each dough onto a floured smooth surface and roll into about 17.5cm round.
5. Place each rolled dough into a quiche pan and press firmly in the bottom and along the edges.
6. Then trim the excess edges.
7. In a small bowl, add the eggs, cream, salt and black pepper and beat until well combined.
8. Place the cream mixture over each crust evenly and top with the salmon, followed by the spring onion.
9. Press either "Zone 1" or "Zone 2" of Instant 2-Basket Air Fryer and then rotate the knob for each zone to select "Air Fry".
10. Set the temperature to 180 degrees C and then set the time for 5 minutes to preheat.
11. After preheating, arrange 1 quiche pan into the basket of each zone.
12. Slide the basket into the Air Fryer and set the time for 20 minutes.
13. After cooking time is completed, remove the quiche pans from Air Fryer.
14. Cut each quiche in 2 portions and serve hot.

Cheesy Scrambled Eggs And Egg And Bacon Muffins

Servings: 3
Cooking Time: 15 Minutes
Ingredients:
- Cheesy Scrambled Eggs:
- 1 teaspoon unsalted butter
- 2 large eggs
- 2 tablespoons milk
- 2 tablespoons shredded Cheddar cheese
- Salt and freshly ground black pepper, to taste
- Egg and Bacon Muffins:
- 2 eggs
- Salt and ground black pepper, to taste
- 1 tablespoon green pesto
- 85 g shredded Cheddar cheese
- 140 g cooked bacon
- 1 spring onion, chopped

Directions:
1. Make the Cheesy Scrambled Eggs :
2. Preheat the zone 1 air fryer basket to 150°C. Place the butter in a baking pan and cook for 1 to 2 minutes, until melted.
3. In a small bowl, whisk together the eggs, milk, and cheese. Season with salt and black pepper. Transfer the mixture to the pan.
4. Cook in the zone 1 basket for 3 minutes. Stir the eggs and push them toward the center of the pan.
5. Cook for another 2 minutes, then stir again. Cook for another 2 minutes, until the eggs are just cooked. Serve warm.
6. Make the Egg and Bacon Muffins :
7. Preheat the zone 2 air fryer basket to 175°C. Line a cupcake tin with parchment paper.
8. Beat the eggs with pepper, salt, and pesto in a bowl. Mix in the cheese.
9. Pour the eggs into the cupcake tin and top with the bacon and spring onion.
10. Bake in the preheated zone 2 air fryer basket for 15 minutes, or until the egg is set.
11. Serve immediately.

Buttermilk Biscuits With Roasted Stone Fruit Compote

Servings: 4
Cooking Time: 20 Minutes
Ingredients:
- FOR THE BISCUITS
- 1⅓ cups all-purpose flour
- 2 teaspoons sugar
- 2 teaspoons baking powder
- ½ teaspoon baking soda
- ½ teaspoon kosher salt
- 4 tablespoons (½ stick) very cold unsalted butter
- ½ cup plus 1 tablespoon low-fat buttermilk
- FOR THE FRUIT COMPOTE
- 2 peaches, peeled and diced
- 2 plums, peeled and diced
- ¼ cup water
- 2 teaspoons honey
- ⅛ teaspoon ground ginger (optional)

Directions:
1. To prep the biscuits: In a small bowl, combine the flour, sugar, baking powder, baking soda, and salt. Using the large holes on a box grater, grate in the butter. Stir in the buttermilk to form a thick dough.
2. Place the dough on a lightly floured surface and gently pat it into a ½-inch-thick disc. Fold the dough in half, then rotate the whole thing 90 degrees, pat into a ½-inch thick disc and fold again. Repeat until you have folded the dough four times.
3. Pat the dough out a final time into a ½-inch-thick disc and use a 3-inch biscuit cutter to cut 4 biscuits from the dough (discard the scraps).
4. To prep the fruit compote: In a large bowl, stir together the peaches, plums, water, honey, and ginger (if using).
5. To cook the biscuits and compote: Install a crisper plate in the Zone 1 basket, place the biscuits in the basket, and insert the basket in the unit. Place the fruit in the Zone 2 basket and insert the basket in the unit.
6. Select Zone 1, select AIR FRY, set the temperature to 400°F, and set the time to 10 minutes.
7. Select Zone 2, select ROAST, set the temperature to 350°F, and set the time to 20 minutes. Select SMART FINISH.
8. Press START/PAUSE to begin cooking.
9. When the Zone 2 timer reads 10 minutes, press START/PAUSE. Remove the basket and stir the compote. Reinsert the basket and press START/PAUSE to resume cooking.
10. When cooking is complete, the biscuits will be golden brown and crisp on top and the fruit will be soft. Transfer the biscuits to a plate to cool. Lightly mash the fruit to form a thick, jammy sauce.
11. Split the biscuits in half horizontally and serve topped with fruit compote.

Nutrition:
- (Per serving) Calories: 332; Total fat: 12g; Saturated fat: 7.5g; Carbohydrates: 50g; Fiber: 2.5g; Protein: 6g; Sodium: 350mg

Baked Peach Oatmeal

Servings: 6
Cooking Time: 30 Minutes
Ingredients:
- Olive oil cooking spray
- 475 ml certified gluten-free rolled oats
- 475 ml unsweetened almond milk
- 60 ml honey, plus more for drizzling (optional)
- 120 ml non-fat plain Greek yoghurt
- 1 teaspoon vanilla extract
- ½ teaspoon ground cinnamon
- ¼ teaspoon salt
- 350 ml diced peaches, divided, plus more for serving (optional)

Directions:
1. Lightly coat the inside of a 6-inch cake pan with olive oil cooking spray. In a large bowl, mix together the oats, almond milk, honey, yoghurt, vanilla, cinnamon, and salt until well combined.
2. Fold in 180 ml peaches and then pour the mixture into the prepared cake pan. Sprinkle the remaining peaches across the top of the oatmeal mixture.
3. Place the cake pan into the zone 1 drawer and bake at 190°C for 30 minutes. Allow to set and cool for 5 minutes before serving with additional fresh fruit and honey for drizzling, if desired.

Buffalo Chicken Breakfast Muffins

Servings: 10
Cooking Time: 13 To 16 Minutes
Ingredients:
- 170 g shredded cooked chicken
- 85 g blue cheese, crumbled
- 2 tablespoons unsalted butter, melted
- 80 ml Buffalo hot sauce, such as Frank's RedHot
- 1 teaspoon minced garlic
- 6 large eggs
- Sea salt and freshly ground black pepper, to taste
- Avocado oil spray

Directions:
1. In a large bowl, stir together the chicken, blue cheese, melted butter, hot sauce, and garlic.
2. In a medium bowl or large liquid measuring cup, beat the eggs. Season with salt and pepper.
3. Spray 10 silicone muffin cups with oil. Divide the chicken mixture among the cups, and pour the egg mixture over top.
4. Place the cups in the two air fryer baskets and set to 150°C. Bake for 13 to 16 minutes, until the muffins are set and cooked through.

Sesame Bagels

Servings: 4
Cooking Time: 15 Minutes
Ingredients:
- 125g self-rising flour
- 240g non-fat plain Greek yoghurt
- 1 beaten egg
- 30g sesame seeds

Directions:
1. Combine the self-rising flour and Greek yoghurt in a medium mixing bowl using a wooden spoon.
2. Knead the dough for about 5 minutes on a lightly floured board.
3. Divide the dough into four equal pieces and roll each into a thin rope, securing the ends to form a bagel shape. Sprinkle the sesame seeds on it.
4. Press either "Zone 1" or "Zone 2" and then rotate the knob to select "Air Fryer".
5. Set the temperature to 140 degrees C, and then set the time for 3 minutes to preheat.
6. After preheating, arrange bagels into the basket.
7. Slide basket into Air Fryer and set the time for 15 minutes.
8. After cooking time is completed, remove both pans from Air Fryer.
9. Place the bagels onto a wire rack to cool for about 10 minutes and serve.

Sausage With Eggs

Servings:2
Cooking Time:13
Ingredients:
- 4 sausage links, raw and uncooked
- 4 eggs, uncooked
- 1 tablespoon of green onion
- 2 tablespoons of chopped tomatoes
- Salt and black pepper, to taste
- 2 tablespoons of milk, dairy
- Oil spray, for greasing

Directions:
1. Take a bowl and whisk eggs in it.
2. Then pour milk, and add onions and tomatoes.
3. Whisk it all well.
4. Now season it with salt and black pepper.
5. Take one cake pan, that fit inside the air fryer and grease it with oil spray.
6. Pour the omelet in the greased cake pans.
7. Put the cake pan inside zone 1 air fryer basket of Instante 2-Basket Air Fryer.
8. Now place the sausage link into the zone 2 basket.
9. Select bake for zone 1 basket and set the timer to 8-10 minutes at 300 degrees F.
10. For the zone 2 basket, select the AIR FRY button and set the timer to 12 minutes at 390 degrees.
11. Once the cooking cycle completes, serve by transferring it to plates.
12. Chop the sausage or cut it in round and then mix it with omelet.
13. Enjoy hot as a delicious breakfast.

Nutrition:
- (Per serving) Calories 240 | Fat 18.4g| Sodium 396mg | Carbs 2.8g | Fiber0.2g | Sugar 2g | Protein 15.6g

Breakfast Sausage And Cauliflower

Servings: 4
Cooking Time: 45 Minutes
Ingredients:
- 450 g sausage meat, cooked and crumbled
- 475 ml double/whipping cream
- 1 head cauliflower, chopped
- 235 ml grated Cheddar cheese, plus more for topping
- 8 eggs, beaten
- Salt and ground black pepper, to taste

Directions:
1. Preheat the air fryer to 176°C.
2. In a large bowl, mix the sausage, cream, chopped cauliflower, cheese and eggs. Sprinkle with salt and ground black pepper.
3. Pour the mixture into a greased casserole dish. Bake in the preheated air fryer for 45 minutes or until firm.
4. Top with more Cheddar cheese and serve.

Breakfast Potatoes

Servings: 6
Cooking Time: 20 Minutes
Ingredients:
- 3 russet potatoes, cut into bite-sized pieces with skin on
- 1 teaspoon garlic powder
- 1 teaspoon onion powder
- 2 teaspoons fine ground sea salt
- 1 teaspoon black pepper
- 1 tablespoon olive oil
- ½ red pepper, diced

Directions:
1. The potatoes should be washed and scrubbed before being sliced into bite-sized pieces with the skin on.
2. Using paper towels, dry them and place them in a large mixing bowl.
3. Toss in the spices and drizzle with olive oil. Stir in the pepper until everything is completely combined.
4. Line a basket with parchment paper.
5. Press either "Zone 1" or "Zone 2" and then rotate the knob to select "Air Fryer".
6. Set the temperature to 195 degrees C, and then set the time for 3 minutes to preheat.
7. After preheating, spread the potatoes in a single layer on the sheet.
8. Slide basket into Air Fryer and set the time for 15 minutes.
9. After cooking time is completed, remove basket from Air Fryer.
10. Place them on serving plates and serve.

Perfect Cinnamon Toast

Servings: 6
Cooking Time: 10 Minutes
Ingredients:
- 12 slices whole-wheat bread
- 1 stick butter, room temperature
- ½ cup white sugar
- 1½ teaspoons ground cinnamon
- 1½ teaspoons pure vanilla extract
- 1 pinch kosher salt
- 2 pinches freshly ground black pepper (optional)

Directions:
1. Mash the softened butter with a fork or the back of a spoon in a bowl. Add the sugar, cinnamon, vanilla, and salt. Stir until everything is well combined.
2. Spread one-sixth of the mixture onto each slice of bread, making sure to cover the entire surface.
3. Install a crisper plate in both drawers. Place half the bread sliced in the zone 1 drawer and half in the zone 2 drawer, then insert the drawers into the unit.
4. Select zone 1, select AIR FRY, set temperature to 400 degrees F/ 200 degrees C, and set time to 5 minutes. Select MATCH to match zone 2 settings to zone 1. Press theSTART/STOP button to begin cooking
5. When cooking is complete, remove the slices and cut them diagonally.
6. Serve immediately.

Nutrition:
- (Per serving) Calories 322 | Fat 16.5g | Sodium 249mg | Carbs 39.3g | Fiber 4.2g | Sugar 18.2g | Protein 8.2g

Cajun Breakfast Sausage

Servings: 8
Cooking Time: 15 To 20 Minutes
Ingredients:
- 680 g 85% lean turkey mince
- 3 cloves garlic, finely chopped
- ¼ onion, grated
- 1 teaspoon Tabasco sauce
- 1 teaspoon Cajun seasoning
- 1 teaspoon dried thyme
- ½ teaspoon paprika
- ½ teaspoon cayenne

Directions:
1. Preheat the air fryer to 188°C.
2. In a large bowl, combine the turkey, garlic, onion, Tabasco, Cajun seasoning, thyme, paprika, and cayenne. Mix with clean hands until thoroughly combined. Shape into 16 patties, about ½ inch thick.
3. Arrange the patties in a single layer in the two air fryer drawers. Pausing halfway through the cooking time to flip the patties, air fry for 15 to 20 minutes until a thermometer inserted into the thickest portion registers 74°C.

Nutty Granola

Servings: 4
Cooking Time: 1 Hour
Ingredients:
- 120 ml pecans, coarsely chopped
- 120 ml walnuts or almonds, coarsely chopped
- 60 ml desiccated coconut
- 60 ml almond flour
- 60 ml ground flaxseed or chia seeds
- 2 tablespoons sunflower seeds
- 2 tablespoons melted butter
- 60 ml granulated sweetener
- ½ teaspoon ground cinnamon
- ½ teaspoon vanilla extract
- ¼ teaspoon ground nutmeg
- ¼ teaspoon salt
- 2 tablespoons water

Directions:
1. Preheat the air fryer to 120°C. Cut a piece of parchment paper to fit inside the air fryer basket.
2. In a large bowl, toss the nuts, coconut, almond flour, ground flaxseed or chia seeds, sunflower seeds, butter, sweetener, cinnamon, vanilla, nutmeg, salt, and water until thoroughly combined.
3. Spread the granola on the parchment paper and flatten to an even thickness.
4. Air fry in the zone 1 air fryer basket for about an hour, or until golden throughout. Remove from the air fryer and allow to fully cool. Break the granola into bite-size pieces and store in a covered container for up to a week.

Sausage And Egg Breakfast Burrito

Servings: 6
Cooking Time: 30 Minutes
Ingredients:
- 6 eggs
- Salt and pepper, to taste
- Cooking oil
- 120 ml chopped red pepper
- 120 ml chopped green pepper
- 230 g chicken sausage meat (removed from casings)
- 120 ml salsa
- 6 medium (8-inch) flour tortillas
- 120 ml shredded Cheddar cheese

Directions:
1. In a medium bowl, whisk the eggs. Add salt and pepper to taste.
2. Place a skillet on medium-high heat. Spray with cooking oil. Add the eggs. Scramble for 2 to 3 minutes, until the eggs are fluffy. Remove the eggs from the skillet and set aside.
3. If needed, spray the skillet with more oil. Add the chopped red and green bell peppers. Cook for 2 to 3 minutes, until the peppers are soft.
4. Add the sausage meat to the skillet. Break the sausage into smaller pieces using a spatula or spoon. Cook for 3 to 4 minutes, until the sausage is brown.
5. Add the salsa and scrambled eggs. Stir to combine. Remove the skillet from heat.
6. Spoon the mixture evenly onto the tortillas.
7. To form the burritos, fold the sides of each tortilla in toward the middle and then roll up from the bottom. You can secure each burrito with a toothpick. Or you can moisten the outside edge of the tortilla with a small amount of water. I prefer to use a cooking brush, but you can also dab with your fingers.
8. Spray the burritos with cooking oil and place them in the two air fryer drawers. Do not stack. Air fry at 204°C for 8 minutes.
9. Open the air fryer and flip the burritos. Cook for an additional 2 minutes or until crisp.
10. Sprinkle the Cheddar cheese over the burritos. Cool before serving.

Parmesan Sausage Egg Muffins

Servings: 4
Cooking Time: 20 Minutes
Ingredients:
- 170 g Italian-seasoned sausage, sliced
- 6 eggs
- 30 ml double cream
- Salt and ground black pepper, to taste
- 85 g Parmesan cheese, grated

Directions:
1. Preheat the air fryer to 176ºC. Grease a muffin pan.
2. Put the sliced sausage in the muffin pan.
3. Beat the eggs with the cream in a bowl and season with salt and pepper.
4. Pour half of the mixture over the sausages in the pan.
5. Sprinkle with cheese and the remaining egg mixture.
6. Bake in the preheated air fryer for 20 minutes or until set.
7. Serve immediately.

Tomato And Mozzarella Bruschetta And Portobello Eggs Benedict

Servings: 3
Cooking Time: 10 To 14 Minutes
Ingredients:
- Tomato and Mozzarella Bruschetta:
- 6 small loaf slices
- 120 ml tomatoes, finely chopped
- 85 g Mozzarella cheese, grated
- 1 tablespoon fresh basil, chopped
- 1 tablespoon olive oil
- Portobello Eggs Benedict:
- 1 tablespoon olive oil
- 2 cloves garlic, minced
- ¼ teaspoon dried thyme
- 2 portobello mushrooms, stems removed and gills scraped out
- 2 plum tomatoes, halved lengthwise
- Salt and freshly ground black pepper, to taste
- 2 large eggs
- 2 tablespoons grated Pecorino Romano cheese
- 1 tablespoon chopped fresh parsley, for garnish
- 1 teaspoon truffle oil (optional)

Directions:
1. Make the Tomato and Mozzarella Bruschetta :
2. Preheat the air fryer to 175ºC.
3. Put the loaf slices inside the zone 1 air fryer basket and air fry for about 3 minutes.
4. Add the tomato, Mozzarella, basil, and olive oil on top.
5. Air fry for an additional minute before serving.
6. Make the Portobello Eggs Benedict :
7. Preheat the air fryer to 205ºC.
8. In a small bowl, combine the olive oil, garlic, and thyme. Brush the mixture over the mushrooms and tomatoes until thoroughly coated. Season to taste with salt and freshly ground black pepper.
9. Arrange the vegetables, cut side up, in the zone 2 air fryer basket. Crack an egg into the center of each mushroom and sprinkle with cheese. Air fry for 10 to 14 minutes until the vegetables are tender and the whites are firm. When cool enough to handle, coarsely chop the tomatoes and place on top of the eggs. Scatter parsley on top and drizzle with truffle oil, if desired, just before serving.

Air Fried Sausage

Servings: 4
Cooking Time: 13 Minutes.
Ingredients:
- 4 sausage links, raw and uncooked

Directions:
1. Divide the sausages in the two crisper plates.
2. Return the crisper plate to the Instant Dual Zone Air Fryer.
3. Choose the Air Fry mode for Zone 1 and set the temperature to 390 degrees F and set the time to 13 minutes.
4. Select the "MATCH" button to copy the settings for Zone 2.
5. Initiate cooking by pressing the START/STOP button.
6. Serve warm and fresh.

Nutrition:
- (Per serving) Calories 267 | Fat 12g |Sodium 165mg | Carbs 39g | Fiber 1.4g | Sugar 22g | Protein 3.3g

Eggs In Avocado Cups

Servings: 4
Cooking Time: 12 Minutes
Ingredients:
- 2 avocados, halved and pitted
- 4 eggs
- Salt and ground black pepper, as required

Directions:
1. Line either basket of "Zone 1" and "Zone 2" of Instant 2-Basket Air Fryer with a greased square piece of foil.
2. Press your chosen zone - "Zone 1" and "Zone 2" and then rotate the knob to select "Bake".
3. Set the temperature to 200 degrees C and then set the time for 5 minutes to preheat.
4. Meanwhile, carefully scoop out about 2 teaspoons of flesh from each avocado half.
5. Crack 1 egg in each avocado half and sprinkle with salt and black pepper.
6. After preheating, arrange 2 avocado halves into the basket.
7. Slide the basket into the Air Fryer and set the time for 12 minutes.
8. After cooking time is completed, transfer the avocado halves and onto serving plates and serve hot.

Cheddar-ham-corn Muffins

Servings: 8 Muffins
Cooking Time: 6 To 8 Minutes
Ingredients:
- 180 ml cornmeal/polenta
- 60 ml flour
- 1½ teaspoons baking powder
- ¼ teaspoon salt
- 1 egg, beaten
- 2 tablespoons rapeseed oil
- 120 ml milk
- 120 ml shredded sharp Cheddar cheese
- 120 ml diced ham
- 8 foil muffin cups, liners removed and sprayed with cooking spray

Directions:
1. Preheat the air fryer to 200ºC.
2. In a medium bowl, stir together the cornmeal, flour, baking powder, and salt.
3. Add egg, oil, and milk to dry ingredients and mix well.
4. Stir in shredded cheese and diced ham.
5. Divide batter among the muffin cups.
6. Place filled muffin cups in two air fryer drawers and bake for 5 minutes.
7. Reduce temperature to 166ºC and bake for 1 to 2 minutes or until toothpick inserted in center of muffin comes out clean.

Canadian Bacon Muffin Sandwiches And All-in-one Toast

Servings: 5
Cooking Time: 10 Minutes
Ingredients:
- Canadian Bacon Muffin Sandwiches:
- 4 English muffins, split
- 8 slices back bacon
- 4 slices cheese
- Cooking spray
- All-in-One Toast:
- 1 strip bacon, diced
- 1 slice 1-inch thick bread
- 1 egg
- Salt and freshly ground black pepper, to taste
- 60 ml grated Monterey Jack or Chedday cheese

Directions:
1. Make the Canadian Bacon Muffin Sandwiches :
2. 1. Preheat the air fryer to 190ºC. Make the sandwiches: Top each of 4 muffin halves with 2 slices of bacon, 1 slice of cheese, and finish with the remaining muffin half. 3. Put the sandwiches in the zone 1 air fryer basket and spritz the tops with cooking spray. 4. Bake for 4 minutes. Flip the sandwiches and bake for another 4 minutes. 5. Divide the sandwiches among four plates and serve warm.
3. Make the All-in-One Toast :
4. Preheat the air fryer to 205ºC.
5. Air fry the bacon in zone 2 basket for 3 minutes, shaking the basket once or twice while it cooks. Remove the bacon to a paper towel lined plate and set aside.
6. Use a sharp paring knife to score a large circle in the middle of the slice of bread, cutting halfway through, but not all the way through to the cutting board. Press down on the circle in the center of the bread slice to create an indentation.
7. Transfer the slice of bread, hole side up, to the zone 2 air fryer basket. Crack the egg into the center of the bread, and season with salt and pepper.
8. Adjust the air fryer temperature to 190ºC and air fry for 5 minutes. Sprinkle the grated cheese around the edges of the bread, leaving the center of the yolk uncovered, and top with the cooked bacon. Press the cheese and bacon into the bread lightly to help anchor it to the bread and prevent it from blowing around in the air fryer.
9. Air fry for one or two more minutes, just to melt the cheese and finish cooking the egg. Serve immediately.

Vegetables And Sides Recipes

Fried Avocado Tacos

Servings: 4
Cooking Time: 10 Minutes
Ingredients:
- For the sauce:
- 2 cups shredded fresh kale or coleslaw mix
- ¼ cup minced fresh cilantro
- ¼ cup plain Greek yogurt
- 2 tablespoons lime juice
- 1 teaspoon honey
- ¼ teaspoon salt
- ¼ teaspoon ground chipotle pepper
- ¼ teaspoon pepper
- For the tacos:
- 1 large egg, beaten
- ¼ cup cornmeal
- ½ teaspoon salt
- ½ teaspoon garlic powder
- ½ teaspoon ground chipotle pepper
- 2 medium avocados, peeled and sliced
- Cooking spray
- 8 flour tortillas or corn tortillas (6 inches), heated up
- 1 medium tomato, chopped
- Crumbled queso fresco (optional)

Directions:
1. Combine the first 8 ingredients in a bowl. Cover and refrigerate until serving.
2. Place the egg in a shallow bowl. In another shallow bowl, mix the cornmeal, salt, garlic powder, and chipotle pepper.
3. Dip the avocado slices in the egg, then into the cornmeal mixture, gently patting to help adhere.
4. Place a crisper plate in both drawers. Put the avocado slices in the drawers in a single layer. Insert the drawers into the unit.
5. Select zone 1, then AIR FRY, then set the temperature to 360 degrees F/ 180 degrees C with a 6-minute timer. To match zone 2 settings to zone 1, choose MATCH. To begin, select START/STOP.
6. Put the avocado slices, prepared sauce, tomato, and queso fresco in the tortillas and serve.

Zucchini With Stuffing

Servings: 3
Cooking Time: 20
Ingredients:
- 1 cup quinoa, rinsed
- 1 cup black olives
- 6 medium zucchinis, about 2 pounds
- 2 cups cannellini beans, drained
- 1 white onion, chopped
- ¼ cup almonds, chopped
- 4 cloves of garlic, chopped
- 4 tablespoons olive oil
- 1 cup of water
- 2 cups Parmesan cheese, for topping

Directions:
1. First wash the zucchini and cut it lengthwise.
2. Take a skillet and heat oil in it
3. Sauté the onion in olive oil for a few minutes.
4. Then add the quinoa and water and let it cook for 8 minutes with the lid on the top.
5. Transfer the quinoa to a bowl and add all remaining ingredients excluding zucchini and Parmesan cheese.
6. Scoop out the seeds of zucchinis.
7. Fill the cavity of zucchinis with bowl mixture.
8. Top it with a handful of Parmesan cheese.
9. Arrange 4 zucchinis in both air fryer baskets.
10. Select zone1 basket at AIR FRY for 20 minutes and adjusting the temperature to 390 degrees F.
11. Use the Match button to select the same setting for zone 2.
12. Serve and enjoy.

Nutrition:
- (Per serving) Calories 1171| Fat 48.6g| Sodium 1747mg | Carbs 132.4g | Fiber 42.1g | Sugar 11.5g | Protein 65.7g

Rosemary Asparagus & Potatoes

Servings: 6
Cooking Time: 30 Minutes
Ingredients:
- 125g asparagus, trimmed & cut into pieces
- 2 tsp garlic powder
- 2 tbsp rosemary, chopped
- 30ml olive oil
- 679g baby potatoes, quartered
- ½ tsp red pepper flakes
- Pepper
- Salt

Directions:
1. Insert a crisper plate in the Instant air fryer baskets.
2. Toss potatoes with 1 tablespoon of oil, pepper, and salt in a bowl until well coated.
3. Add potatoes into in zone 1 basket.
4. Toss asparagus with remaining oil, red pepper flakes, pepper, garlic powder, and rosemary in a mixing bowl.
5. Add asparagus into the zone 2 basket.
6. Select zone 1, then select "air fry" mode and set the temperature to 390 degrees F for 20 minutes. Select zone 2, then select "air fry" mode and set the temperature to 390 degrees F for 10 minutes. Press "match" mode, then press "start/stop" to begin.

Nutrition:
- (Per serving) Calories 121 | Fat 5g |Sodium 40mg | Carbs 17.1g | Fiber 4.2g | Sugar 1g | Protein 4g

Kale And Spinach Chips

Servings: 2
Cooking Time: 6 Minutes
Ingredients:
- 2 cups spinach, torn in pieces and stem removed
- 2 cups kale, torn in pieces, stems removed
- 1 tablespoon olive oil
- Sea salt, to taste
- ⅓ cup Parmesan cheese

Directions:
1. Take a bowl and add spinach to it.
2. Take another bowl and add kale to it.
3. Season both of them with olive oil and sea salt.
4. Add the kale to the zone 1 basket and spinach to the zone 2 basket.
5. Select AIR FRY mode for zone 1 at 350 degrees F/ 175 degrees C for 6 minutes.
6. Set zone 2 to AIR FRY mode at 350 degrees F/ 175 degrees C for 5 minutes.
7. Once done, take out the crispy chips and sprinkle Parmesan cheese on top. 8. Serve and Enjoy.

Buffalo Bites

Servings: 6
Cooking Time: 30 Minutes
Ingredients:
- For the bites:
- 1 small cauliflower head, cut into florets
- 2 tablespoons olive oil
- 3 tablespoons buffalo wing sauce
- 3 tablespoons butter, melted
- For the dip:
- 1½ cups 2% cottage cheese
- ¼ cup fat-free plain Greek yogurt
- ¼ cup crumbled blue cheese
- 1 sachet ranch salad dressing mix
- Celery sticks (optional)

Directions:
1. In a large bowl, combine the cauliflower and oil| toss to coat.
2. Place a crisper plate in each drawer. Put the coated cauliflower florets in each drawer in a single layer. Place the drawers in the unit.
3. Select zone 1, then AIR FRY, then set the temperature to 360 degrees F/ 180 degrees C with a 15-minute timer. To match zone 2 settings to zone 1, choose MATCH. To begin, select START/STOP.
4. Remove the cauliflower from the drawers after the timer has finished.
5. Combine the buffalo sauce and melted butter in a large mixing bowl. Put in the cauliflower and toss to coat. Place on a serving dish and serve.
6. Combine the dip ingredients in a small bowl. Serve with the cauliflower and celery sticks, if desired.

Fried Asparagus

Servings: 4
Cooking Time: 6 Minutes
Ingredients:
- ¼ cup mayonnaise
- 4 teaspoons olive oil
- 1½ teaspoons grated lemon zest
- 1 garlic clove, minced
- ½ teaspoon pepper
- ¼ teaspoon seasoned salt
- 1-pound fresh asparagus, trimmed
- 2 tablespoons shredded parmesan cheese
- Lemon wedges (optional)

Directions:
1. In a large bowl, combine the first 6 ingredients.
2. Add the asparagus| toss to coat.
3. Put a crisper plate in both drawers. Put the asparagus in a single layer in each drawer. Top with the parmesan cheese. Place the drawers into the unit.
4. Select zone 1, then AIR FRY, then set the temperature to 375 degrees F/ 190 degrees C with a 6-minute timer. To match zone 2 settings to zone 1, choose MATCH. To begin, select START/STOP.
5. Remove the asparagus from the drawers after the timer has finished.

Acorn Squash Slices

Servings: 6
Cooking Time: 10 Minutes
Ingredients:
- 2 medium acorn squashes
- ⅔ cup packed brown sugar
- ½ cup butter, melted

Directions:
1. Cut the squash in half, remove the seeds and slice into ½ inch slices.
2. Place the squash slices in the air fryer baskets.
3. Drizzle brown sugar and butter over the squash slices.
4. Return the air fryer basket 1 to Zone 1, and basket 2 to Zone 2 of the Instant 2-Basket Air Fryer.
5. Choose the "Air Fry" mode for Zone 1 and set the temperature to 350 degrees F and 10 minutes of cooking time.
6. Select the "MATCH COOK" option to copy the settings for Zone 2.
7. Initiate cooking by pressing the START/PAUSE BUTTON.
8. Flip the squash once cooked halfway through.
9. Serve.

Nutrition:
- (Per serving) Calories 206 | Fat 3.4g |Sodium 174mg | Carbs 35g | Fiber 9.4g | Sugar 5.9g | Protein 10.6g

Stuffed Sweet Potatoes

Servings: 4
Cooking Time: 55 Minutes
Ingredients:
- 2 medium sweet potatoes
- 1 teaspoon olive oil
- 1 cup cooked chopped spinach, drained
- 1 cup shredded cheddar cheese, divided
- 2 cooked bacon strips, crumbled
- 1 green onion, chopped
- ¼ cup fresh cranberries, coarsely chopped
- ⅓ cup chopped pecans, toasted
- 2 tablespoons butter
- ¼ teaspoon kosher salt
- ¼ teaspoon pepper

Directions:
1. Brush the sweet potatoes with the oil.
2. Place a crisper plate in both drawers. Add one sweet potato to each drawer. Place the drawers in the unit.
3. Select zone 1, then AIR FRY, then set the temperature to 360 degrees F/ 180 degrees C with a 40-minute timer. To match zone 2 settings to zone 1, choose MATCH. To begin, select START/STOP.
4. Remove the sweet potatoes from the drawers after the timer has finished. Cut them in half lengthwise. Scoop out the pulp, leaving a ¼-inch thick shell. 5. Put the pulp in a large bowl and stir in the spinach, ¾ cup of cheese, bacon, onion, pecans, cranberries, butter, salt, and pepper.
5. Spoon the mixture into the potato shells, mounding the mixture slightly.
6. Place a crisper plate in each drawer. Put one filled potato into each drawer and insert them into the unit.
7. Select zone 1, then AIR FRY, then set the temperature to 360 degrees F/ 180 degrees C with a 10-minute timer. To match zone 2 settings to zone 1, choose MATCH. To begin, select START/STOP.
8. Sprinkle with the remaining ¼ cup of cheese. Cook using the same settings until the cheese is melted.

Green Salad With Crispy Fried Goat Cheese And Baked Croutons

Servings: 4
Cooking Time: 10 Minutes
Ingredients:
- FOR THE GOAT CHEESE
- 1 (4-ounce) log soft goat cheese
- ½ cup panko bread crumbs
- 2 tablespoons vegetable oil
- FOR THE CROUTONS
- 2 slices Italian-style sandwich bread
- 2 tablespoons vegetable oil
- 1 tablespoon poultry seasoning
- ½ teaspoon kosher salt
- ¼ teaspoon freshly ground black pepper
- FOR THE SALAD
- 8 cups green leaf lettuce leaves
- ½ cup store-bought balsamic vinaigrette

Directions:
1. To prep the goat cheese: Cut the goat cheese into 8 round slices.
2. Spread the panko on a plate. Gently press the cheese into the panko to coat on both sides. Drizzle with the oil.
3. To prep the croutons: Cut the bread into cubes and place them in a large bowl. Add the oil, poultry seasoning, salt, and black pepper. Mix well to coat the bread cubes evenly.
4. To cook the goat cheese and croutons: Install a crisper plate in each of the two baskets. Place the goat cheese in the Zone 1 basket and insert the basket in the unit. Place the croutons in the Zone 2 basket and insert the basket in the unit.
5. Select Zone 1, select AIR FRY, set the temperature to 400°F, and set the timer to 6 minutes.
6. Select Zone 2, select BAKE, set the temperature to 390°F, and set the timer to 10 minutes. Select SMART FINISH.
7. Press START/PAUSE to begin cooking.
8. When cooking is complete, the goat cheese will be golden brown and the croutons crisp.
9. Remove the Zone 1 basket. Let the goat cheese cool in the basket for 5 minutes; it will firm up as it cools.
10. To assemble the salad: In a large bowl, combine the lettuce, vinaigrette, and croutons. Toss well. Divide the salad among four plates. Top each plate with 2 pieces of goat cheese.

Nutrition:
- (Per serving) Calories: 578; Total fat: 40g; Saturated fat: 14g; Carbohydrates: 39g; Fiber: 3.5g; Protein: 24g; Sodium: 815mg

GGarlic-rosemary Brussels Sprouts

Servings: 4
Cooking Time: 15 Minutes
Ingredients:
- 3 tablespoons olive oil
- 2 garlic cloves, minced
- ½ teaspoon salt
- ¼ teaspoon pepper
- 1-pound Brussels sprouts, trimmed and halved
- ½ cup panko breadcrumbs
- 1½ teaspoons minced fresh rosemary

Directions:
1. Place the first 4 ingredients in a small microwave-safe bowl| microwave on high for 30 seconds.
2. Toss the Brussels sprouts in 2 tablespoons of the microwaved mixture.
3. Place a crisper plate in each drawer. Put the sprouts in a single layer in each drawer. Insert the drawers into the units.
4. Select zone 1, then AIR FRY, then set the temperature to 360 degrees F/ 180 degrees C with a 6-minute timer. To match zone 2 settings to zone 1, choose MATCH. To begin, select START/STOP.
5. Remove the sprouts from the drawers after the timer has finished.
6. Toss the breadcrumbs with the rosemary and remaining oil mixture| sprinkle over the sprouts.
7. Continue cooking until the crumbs are browned, and the sprouts are tender . Serve immediately.

arlic-herb Fried Squash

Servings: 4
Cooking Time: 15 Minutes
Ingredients:
- 5 cups halved small pattypan squash (about 1¼ pounds)
- 1 tablespoon olive oil
- 2 garlic cloves, minced
- ½ teaspoon salt
- ¼ teaspoon dried oregano
- ¼ teaspoon dried thyme
- ¼ teaspoon pepper
- 1 tablespoon minced fresh parsley, for serving

Directions:
1. Place the squash in a large bowl.
2. Mix the oil, garlic, salt, oregano, thyme, and pepper| drizzle over the squash. Toss to coat.
3. Place a crisper plate in both drawers. Put the squash in a single layer in each drawer. Insert the drawers into the unit.
4. Select zone 1, then AIR FRY, then set the temperature to 360 degrees F/ 180 degrees C with a 6-minute timer. To match zone 2 settings to zone 1, choose MATCH. To begin, select START/STOP.
5. Remove the squash from the drawers after the timer has finished. Sprinkle with the parsley.

Fried Artichoke Hearts

Servings: 6
Cooking Time: 10 Minutes
Ingredients:
- 3 cans Quartered Artichokes, drained
- ½ cup mayonnaise
- 1 cup panko breadcrumbs
- ⅓ cup grated Parmesan
- salt and black pepper to taste
- Parsley for garnish

Directions:
1. Mix mayonnaise with salt and black pepper and keep the sauce aside.
2. Spread panko breadcrumbs in a bowl.
3. Coat the artichoke pieces with the breadcrumbs.
4. As you coat the artichokes, place them in the two crisper plates in a single layer, then spray them with cooking oil.
5. Return the crisper plates to the Instant Dual Zone Air Fryer.
6. Choose the Air Fry mode for Zone 1 and set the temperature to 375 degrees F/ 190 degrees C and the time to 10 minutes.
7. Select the "MATCH" button to copy the settings for Zone 2.
8. Initiate cooking by pressing the START/STOP button.
9. Flip the artichokes once cooked halfway through, then resume cooking.
10. Serve warm with mayo sauce.

Balsamic Vegetables

Servings: 4
Cooking Time: 13 Minutes
Ingredients:
- 125g asparagus, cut woody ends
- 88g mushrooms, halved
- 1 tbsp Dijon mustard
- 3 tbsp soy sauce
- 27g brown sugar
- 57ml balsamic vinegar
- 32g olive oil
- 1 zucchini, sliced
- 1 yellow squash, sliced
- 170g grape tomatoes
- Pepper
- Salt

Directions:
1. In a bowl, mix asparagus, tomatoes, oil, mustard, soy sauce, mushrooms, zucchini, squash, brown sugar, vinegar, pepper, and salt.
2. Cover the bowl and place it in the refrigerator for 45 minutes.
3. Insert a crisper plate in the Instant air fryer baskets.
4. Add the vegetable mixture in both baskets.
5. Select zone 1, then select "air fry" mode and set the temperature to 390 degrees F for 12 minutes. Press "match" to match zone 2 settings to zone 1. Press "start/stop" to begin. Stir halfway through.

Nutrition:
- (Per serving) Calories 184 | Fat 13.3g |Sodium 778mg | Carbs 14.7g | Fiber 3.6g | Sugar 9.5g | Protein 5.5g

Caprese Panini With Zucchini Chips

Servings: 4
Cooking Time: 20 Minutes
Ingredients:
- FOR THE PANINI
- 4 tablespoons pesto
- 8 slices Italian-style sandwich bread
- 1 tomato, diced
- 6 ounces fresh mozzarella cheese, shredded
- ¼ cup mayonnaise
- FOR THE ZUCCHINI CHIPS
- ½ cup all-purpose flour
- 2 large eggs
- ¼ teaspoon freshly ground black pepper
- ⅛ teaspoon kosher salt
- ½ cup panko bread crumbs
- ¼ cup grated Parmesan cheese
- 1 teaspoon Italian seasoning
- 1 medium zucchini, cut into ¼-inch-thick rounds
- 2 tablespoons vegetable oil

Directions:
1. To prep the panini: Spread 1 tablespoon of pesto each on 4 slices of the bread. Layer the diced tomato and shredded mozzarella on the other 4 slices of bread. Top the tomato/cheese mixture with the pesto-coated bread, pesto-side down, to form 4 sandwiches.
2. Spread the outside of each sandwich (both bread slices) with a thin layer of the mayonnaise.
3. To prep the zucchini chips: Set up a breading station with three small shallow bowls. Place the flour in the first bowl. In the second bowl, beat together the eggs, salt, and black pepper. Place the panko, Parmesan, and Italian seasoning in the third bowl.
4. Bread the zucchini in this order: First, dip the slices into the flour, coating both sides. Then, dip into the beaten egg. Finally, coat in the panko mixture. Drizzle the zucchini on both sides with the oil.
5. To cook the panini and zucchini chips: Install a crisper plate in each of the two baskets. Place 2 sandwiches in the Zone 1 basket and insert the basket in the unit. Place half of the zucchini chips in a single layer in the Zone 2 basket and insert the basket in the unit.
6. Select Zone 1, select AIR FRY, set the temperature to 375°F, and set the timer to 20 minutes.
7. Select Zone 2, select AIR FRY, set the temperature to 400°F, and set the timer to 20 minutes. Select SMART FINISH.
8. Press START/PAUSE to begin cooking.
9. When the Zone 1 timer reads 15 minutes, press START/PAUSE. Remove the basket, and use silicone-tipped tongs or a spatula to flip the sandwiches. Reinsert the basket and press START/PAUSE to resume cooking.
10. When both timers read 10 minutes, press START/PAUSE. Remove the Zone 1 basket and transfer the sandwiches to a plate. Place the remaining 2 sandwiches into the basket and insert the basket in the unit. Remove the Zone 2 basket and transfer the zucchini chips to a serving plate. Place the remaining zucchini chips in the basket. Reinsert the basket and press START/PAUSE to resume cooking.
11. When the Zone 1 timer reads 5 minutes, press START/PAUSE. Remove the basket and flip the sandwiches. Reinsert the basket and press START/PAUSE to resume cooking.
12. When cooking is complete, the panini should be toasted and the zucchini chips golden brown and crisp.
13. Cut each panini in half. Serve hot with zucchini chips on the side.

Nutrition:
- (Per serving) Calories: 751; Total fat: 39g; Saturated fat: 9.5g; Carbohydrates: 77g; Fiber: 3.5g; Protein: 23g; Sodium: 1,086mg

Bacon Wrapped Corn Cob

Servings: 4
Cooking Time: 10 Minutes
Ingredients:
- 4 trimmed corns on the cob
- 8 bacon slices

Directions:
1. Wrap the corn cobs with two bacon slices.
2. Place the wrapped cobs into the Instant 2 Baskets Air Fryer baskets.
3. Return the air fryer basket 1 to Zone 1, and basket 2 to Zone 2 of the Instant 2-Basket Air Fryer.
4. Choose the "Air Fry" mode for Zone 1 and set the temperature to 355 degrees F and 10 minutes of cooking time.
5. Select the "MATCH COOK" option to copy the settings for Zone 2.
6. Initiate cooking by pressing the START/PAUSE BUTTON.
7. Flip the corn cob once cooked halfway through.
8. Serve warm.

Nutrition:
- (Per serving) Calories 350 | Fat 2.6g | Sodium 358mg | Carbs 64.6g | Fiber 14.4g | Sugar 3.3g | Protein 19.9g

Buffalo Seitan With Crispy Zucchini Noodles

Servings: 4
Cooking Time: 12 Minutes

Ingredients:
- FOR THE BUFFALO SEITAN
- 1 (8-ounce) package precooked seitan strips
- 1 teaspoon garlic powder, divided
- ½ teaspoon onion powder
- ¼ teaspoon smoked paprika
- ¼ cup Louisiana-style hot sauce
- 2 tablespoons vegetable oil
- 1 tablespoon tomato paste
- ¼ teaspoon freshly ground black pepper
- FOR THE ZUCCHINI NOODLES
- 3 large egg whites
- 1¼ cups all-purpose flour
- 1 teaspoon kosher salt, divided
- 12 ounces seltzer water or club soda
- 5 ounces zucchini noodles
- Nonstick cooking spray

Directions:
1. To prep the Buffalo seitan: Season the seitan strips with ½ teaspoon of garlic powder, the onion powder, and smoked paprika.
2. In a large bowl, whisk together the hot sauce, oil, tomato paste, remaining ½ teaspoon of garlic powder, and the black pepper. Set the bowl of Buffalo sauce aside.
3. To prep the zucchini noodles: In a medium bowl, use a handheld mixer to beat the egg whites until stiff peaks form.
4. In a large bowl, combine the flour and ½ teaspoon of salt. Mix in the seltzer to form a thin batter. Fold in the beaten egg whites.
5. Add the zucchini to the batter and gently mix to coat.
6. To cook the seitan and zucchini noodles: Install a crisper plate in each of the two baskets. Place the seitan in the Zone 1 basket and insert the basket in the unit. Lift the noodles from the batter one at a time, letting the excess drip off, and place them in the Zone 2 basket. Insert the basket in the unit.
7. Select Zone 1, select BAKE, set the temperature to 370°F, and set the timer to 12 minutes.
8. Select Zone 2, select AIR FRY, set the temperature to 400°F, and set the timer to 12 minutes. Select SMART FINISH.
9. Press START/PAUSE to begin cooking.
10. When the Zone 1 timer reads 2 minutes, press START/PAUSE. Remove the basket and transfer the seitan to the bowl of Buffalo sauce. Turn to coat, then return the seitan to the basket. Reinsert the basket and press START/PAUSE to resume cooking.
11. When cooking is complete, the seitan should be warmed through and the zucchini noodles crisp and light golden brown.
12. Sprinkle the zucchini noodles with the remaining ½ teaspoon of salt. If desired, drizzle extra Buffalo sauce over the seitan. Serve hot.

Nutrition:
- (Per serving) Calories: 252; Total fat: 15g; Saturated fat: 1g; Carbohydrates: 22g; Fiber: 1.5g; Protein: 13g; Sodium: 740mg

Potatoes & Beans

Servings: 4
Cooking Time: 25 Minutes

Ingredients:
- 453g potatoes, cut into pieces
- 15ml olive oil
- 1 tsp garlic powder
- 160g green beans, trimmed
- Pepper
- Salt

Directions:
1. In a bowl, toss green beans, garlic powder, potatoes, oil, pepper, and salt.
2. Insert a crisper plate in the Instant air fryer baskets.
3. Add green beans and potato mixture to both baskets.
4. Select zone 1 then select "air fry" mode and set the temperature to 380 degrees F for 25 minutes. Press "match" to match zone 2 settings to zone 1. Press "start/stop" to begin. Stir halfway through.

Nutrition:
- (Per serving) Calories 128 | Fat 3.7g | Sodium 49mg | Carbs 22.4g | Fiber 4.7g | Sugar 2.3g | Protein 3.1g

Potato And Parsnip Latkes With Baked Apples

Servings: 4
Cooking Time: 20 Minutes
Ingredients:
- FOR THE LATKES
- 2 medium russet potatoes, peeled
- 1 large egg white
- 2 tablespoons all-purpose flour
- ¼ teaspoon garlic powder
- ¼ teaspoon kosher salt
- ¼ teaspoon freshly ground black pepper
- 1 medium parsnip, peeled and shredded
- 2 scallions, thinly sliced
- 2 tablespoons vegetable oil
- FOR THE BAKED APPLES
- 2 Golden Delicious apples, peeled and diced
- 2 tablespoons granulated sugar
- 2 teaspoons unsalted butter, cut into small pieces

Directions:
1. To prep the latkes: Grate the potatoes using the large holes of a box grater. Squeeze as much liquid out of the potatoes as you can into a large bowl. Set the potatoes aside in a separate bowl.
2. Let the potato liquid sit for 5 minutes, during which time the potato starch will settle to the bottom of the bowl. Pour off the water that has risen to the top, leaving the potato starch in the bowl.
3. Add the egg white, flour, salt, and black pepper to the potato starch to form a thick paste. Add the potatoes, parsnip, and scallions and mix well. Divide the mixture into 4 patties. Brush both sides of each patty with the oil.
4. To prep the baked apples: Place the apples in the Zone 2 basket. Sprinkle the sugar and butter over the top.
5. To cook the latkes and apples: Install a crisper plate in the Zone 1 basket. Place the latkes in the basket in a single layer, then insert the basket in the unit. Insert the Zone 2 basket in the unit.
6. Select Zone 1, select AIR FRY, set the temperature to 375°F, and set the timer to 15 minutes.
7. Select Zone 2, select BAKE, set the temperature to 330°F, and set the timer to 20 minutes. Select SMART FINISH.
8. Press START/PAUSE to begin cooking.
9. When both timers read 5 minutes, press START/PAUSE. Remove the Zone 1 basket and use silicone-tipped tongs or a spatula to flip the latkes. Reinsert the basket in the unit. Remove the Zone 2 basket and gently mash the apples with a fork or the back of a spoon. Reinsert the basket and press START/PAUSE to resume cooking.
10. When cooking is complete, the latkes should be golden brown and cooked through and the apples very soft.
11. Transfer the latkes to a plate and serve with apples on the side.

Nutrition:
- (Per serving) Calories: 257; Total fat: 9g; Saturated fat: 2g; Carbohydrates: 42g; Fiber: 5.5g; Protein: 4g; Sodium: 91mg

Green Beans With Baked Potatoes

Servings: 2
Cooking Time: 45 Minutes
Ingredients:
- 2 cups green beans
- 2 large potatoes, cubed
- 3 tablespoons olive oil
- 1 teaspoon seasoned salt
- ½ teaspoon chili powder
- ⅙ teaspoon garlic powder
- ¼ teaspoon onion powder

Directions:
1. Take a large bowl and pour olive oil into it.
2. Add all the seasoning in the olive oil and whisk it well.
3. Toss the green beans in and mix well and then transfer to zone 1 basket of the air fryer.
4. Season the potatoes with the oil seasoning and add them to the zone 2 basket.
5. Press the Sync button.
6. Once the cooking cycle is complete, take out and serve.

Falafel

Servings: 6
Cooking Time: 14 Minutes
Ingredients:
- 1 (15.5-oz) can chickpeas, rinsed and drained
- 1 small yellow onion, cut into quarters
- 3 garlic cloves, chopped
- ⅓ cup parsley, chopped
- ⅓ cup cilantro, chopped
- ⅓ cup scallions, chopped
- 1 teaspoon cumin
- ½ teaspoons salt
- ⅛ teaspoons crushed red pepper flakes
- 1 teaspoon baking powder
- 4 tablespoons all-purpose flour
- Olive oil spray

Directions:
1. Dry the chickpeas on paper towels.
2. Add onions and garlic to a food processor and chop them.
3. Add the parsley, salt, cilantro, scallions, cumin, and red pepper flakes.
4. Press the pulse button for 60 seconds, then toss in chickpeas and blend for 3 times until it makes a chunky paste.
5. Stir in baking powder and flour and mix well.
6. Transfer the falafel mixture to a bowl and cover to refrigerate for 3 hours.
7. Make 12 balls out of the falafel mixture.
8. Place 6 falafels in each of the crisper plate and spray them with oil.
9. Return the crisper plate to the Instant Dual Zone Air Fryer.
10. Choose the Air Fry mode for Zone 1 and set the temperature to 350 degrees F/ 175 degrees C and the time to 14 minutes.
11. Select the "MATCH" button to copy the settings for Zone 2.
12. Initiate cooking by pressing the START/STOP button.
13. Toss the falafel once cooked halfway through, and resume cooking.
14. Serve warm.

Fish And Seafood Recipes

Buttered Mahi-mahi

Servings: 4
Cooking Time: 22 Minutes
Ingredients:
- 4 (6-oz) mahi-mahi fillets
- Salt and black pepper ground to taste
- Cooking spray
- ⅔ cup butter

Directions:
1. Preheat your Instant Dual Zone Air Fryer to 350 degrees F.
2. Rub the mahi-mahi fillets with salt and black pepper.
3. Place two mahi-mahi fillets in each of the crisper plate.
4. Return the crisper plates to the Instant Dual Zone Air Fryer.
5. Choose the Air Fry mode for Zone 1 and set the temperature to 390 degrees F and the time to 17 minutes|
6. Select the "MATCH" button to copy the settings for Zone 2.
7. Initiate cooking by pressing the START/STOP button.
8. Add butter to a saucepan and cook for 5 minutes until slightly brown.
9. Remove the butter from the heat.
10. Drizzle butter over the fish and serve warm.

Chili Honey Salmon

Servings: 2
Cooking Time: 12 Minutes
Ingredients:
- 2 salmon fillets
- 3 tbsp honey
- 1/2 tbsp chili flakes
- 1/2 tsp chili powder
- 1/2 tsp turmeric
- 1 tsp ground coriander
- 1/8 tsp pepper
- 1/8 tsp salt

Directions:
1. Add honey to microwave-safe bowl and heat for 10 seconds.
2. Add chili flakes, chili powder, turmeric, coriander, pepper, and salt into the honey and mix well.
3. Brush salmon fillets with honey mixture.
4. Place salmon fillets into the air fryer basket and cook at 400 F for 12 minutes.
5. Serve and enjoy.

Tuna Patties With Spicy Sriracha Sauce Coconut Prawns

Servings: 6
Cooking Time: 10 Minutes
Ingredients:
- Tuna Patties with Spicy Sriracha Sauce:
- 2 (170 g) cans tuna packed in oil, drained
- 3 tablespoons almond flour
- 2 tablespoons mayonnaise
- 1 teaspoon dried dill
- ½ teaspoon onion powder
- Pinch of salt and pepper
- Spicy Sriracha Sauce:
- 60 g mayonnaise
- 1 tablespoon Sriracha sauce
- 1 teaspoon garlic powder
- Coconut Prawns:
- 230 g medium prawns, peeled and deveined
- 2 tablespoons salted butter, melted
- ½ teaspoon Old Bay seasoning
- 25 g desiccated, unsweetened coconut

Directions:
1. Make the Tuna Patties with Spicy Sriracha Sauce :
2. 1. Preheat the air fryer to 192°C. Line the zone 1 drawer with baking paper. In a large bowl, combine the tuna, almond flour, mayonnaise, dill, and onion powder. Season to taste with salt and freshly ground black pepper. Use a fork to stir, mashing with the back of the fork as necessary, until thoroughly combined. 3. Use an ice cream scoop to form the tuna mixture patties. Place the patties in a single layer on the baking paper in the zone 1 air fryer drawer. Press lightly with the bottom of the scoop to flatten into a circle about ½ inch thick. Pausing halfway through the cooking time to turn the patties, air fry for 10 minutes until lightly browned. 4. To make the Sriracha sauce: In a small bowl, combine the mayonnaise, Sriracha, and garlic powder. Serve the tuna patties topped with the Sriracha sauce.
3. Make the Coconut Prawns :
4. In a large bowl, toss the prawns in butter and Old Bay seasoning.
5. Place shredded coconut in bowl. Coat each piece of prawns in the coconut and place into the zone 2 air fryer drawer.
6. Adjust the temperature to 204°C and air fry for 6 minutes.
7. Gently turn the prawns halfway through the cooking time. Serve immediately.

Tender Juicy Honey Glazed Salmon

Servings: 4
Cooking Time: 10 Minutes
Ingredients:
- 4 salmon fillets
- 1 tbsp honey
- 1/2 tsp red chili flakes, crushed
- 1 tsp sesame seeds, toasted
- 1 1/2 tsp olive oil
- 1 tbsp coconut aminos
- Pepper
- Salt

Directions:
1. Place salmon fillets into the bowl. In a small bowl, mix coconut aminos, oil, pepper, and salt and pour over fish fillets. Mix well.
2. Cover bowl and place in the refrigerator for 20 minutes.
3. Preheat the air fryer to 400 F.
4. Place marinated salmon fillets into the air fryer basket and cook for 8 minutes.
5. Brush fish fillets with honey and sprinkle with chili flakes and sesame seeds and cook for 2 minutes more.
6. Serve and enjoy.

Lemon Butter Salmon

Servings: 2
Cooking Time: 12 Minutes
Ingredients:
- 2 salmon fillets
- 1/2 tsp soy sauce
- 3/4 tsp dill, chopped
- 1 tsp garlic, minced
- 1 1/2 tbsp fresh lemon juice
- 2 tbsp butter, melted
- Pepper
- Salt

Directions:
1. Preheat the air fryer to 400 F.
2. In a small bowl, mix butter, lemon juice, garlic, dill, soy sauce, pepper, and salt.
3. Brush salmon fillets with butter mixture and place into the air fryer basket and cook for 10-12 minutes.
4. Pour the remaining butter mixture over cooked salmon fillets and serve.

Tandoori Prawns

Servings: 4
Cooking Time: 6 Minutes
Ingredients:
- 455 g jumbo raw prawns (21 to 25 count), peeled and deveined
- 1 tablespoon minced fresh ginger
- 3 cloves garlic, minced
- 5 g chopped fresh coriander or parsley, plus more for garnish
- 1 teaspoon ground turmeric
- 1 teaspoon garam masala
- 1 teaspoon smoked paprika
- 1 teaspoon kosher or coarse sea salt
- ½ to 1 teaspoon cayenne pepper
- 2 tablespoons olive oil (for Paleo) or melted ghee
- 2 teaspoons fresh lemon juice

Directions:
1. In a large bowl, combine the prawns, ginger, garlic, coriander, turmeric, garam masala, paprika, salt, and cayenne. Toss well to coat. Add the oil or ghee and toss again. Marinate at room temperature for 15 minutes, or cover and refrigerate for up to 8 hours.
2. Place the prawns in a single layer in the two air fryer baskets. Set the air fryer to 165ºC for 6 minutes. Transfer the prawns to a serving platter. Cover and let the prawns finish cooking in the residual heat, about 5 minutes.
3. Sprinkle the prawns with the lemon juice and toss to coat. Garnish with additional cilantro and serve.

Pretzel-crusted Catfish

Servings: 4
Cooking Time: 12 Minutes
Ingredients:
- 4 catfish fillets
- ½ teaspoon salt
- ½ teaspoon black pepper
- 2 large eggs
- ⅓ cup Dijon mustard
- 2 tablespoons 2% milk
- ½ cup all-purpose flour
- 4 cups miniature pretzels, crushed
- Cooking spray
- Lemon slices

Directions:
1. Rub the catfish with black pepper and salt.
2. Beat eggs with milk and mustard in a bowl.
3. Spread pretzels and flour in two separate bowls.
4. Coat the catfish with flour then dip in the egg mixture and coat with the pretzels.
5. Place two fish fillets in each air fryer basket.
6. Return the air fryer basket 1 to Zone 1, and basket 2 to Zone 2 of the Instant 2-Basket Air Fryer.
7. Choose the "Air Fry" mode for Zone 1 at 325 degrees F and 12 minutes of cooking time.
8. Select the "MATCH COOK" option to copy the settings for Zone 2.
9. Initiate cooking by pressing the START/PAUSE BUTTON.
10. Serve warm.

Nutrition:
- (Per serving) Calories 196 | Fat 7.1g | Sodium 492mg | Carbs 21.6g | Fiber 2.9g | Sugar 0.8g | Protein 13.4g

Fish And Chips

Servings: 2
Cooking Time: 22
Ingredients:
- 1 pound of potatoes, cut lengthwise
- 1 cup seasoned flour
- 2 eggs, organic
- 1/3 cup buttermilk
- 2 cup seafood fry mix
- ½ cup bread crumbs
- 2 codfish fillet, 6 ounces each
- Oil spray, for greasing

Directions:
1. take a bowl and whisk eggs in it along buttermilk.
2. In a separate bowl mix seafood fry mix and bread crumbs
3. Take a baking tray and spread flour on it
4. Dip the fillets first in egg wash, then in flour, and at the end coat it with breadcrumbs mixture.
5. Put the fish fillet in air fryer zone 1 basket.
6. Grease the fish fillet with oil spray.
7. Set zone 1 to AIR FRY mode at 400 degrees F for 14 minutes.
8. Put potato chip in zone two baskets and lightly grease it with oil spray.
9. Set the zone 2 basket to AIRFRY mode at 400 degrees F for 22 minutes.
10. Hit the smart finish button.
11. Once done, serve and enjoy.

Nutrition:
- (Per serving) Calories 992| Fat 22.3g| Sodium 1406 mg | Carbs 153.6g | Fiber 10g | Sugar 10 g | Protein 40g

"fried" Fish With Seasoned Potato Wedges

Servings: 4
Cooking Time: 30 Minutes
Ingredients:
- FOR THE FISH
- 4 cod fillets (6 ounces each)
- 4 tablespoons all-purpose flour, divided
- ¼ cup cornstarch
- 1 teaspoon baking powder
- ¼ teaspoon kosher salt
- ⅓ cup lager-style beer or sparkling water
- Tartar sauce, cocktail sauce, or malt vinegar, for serving (optional)
- FOR THE POTATOES
- 4 russet potatoes
- 2 tablespoons vegetable oil
- ½ teaspoon paprika
- ½ teaspoon kosher salt
- ¼ teaspoon garlic powder
- ¼ teaspoon freshly ground black pepper

Directions:
1. To prep the fish: Pat the fish dry with a paper towel and coat lightly with 2 tablespoons of flour.
2. In a shallow dish, combine the remaining 2 tablespoons of flour, the cornstarch, baking powder, and salt. Stir in the beer to form a thick batter.
3. Dip the fish in the batter to coat both sides, then let rest on a cutting board for 10 minutes.
4. To prep the potatoes: Cut each potato in half lengthwise, then cut each half into 4 wedges.
5. In a large bowl, combine the potatoes and oil. Toss well to fully coat the potatoes. Add the paprika, salt, garlic powder, and black pepper and toss well to coat.
6. To cook the fish and potato wedges: Install a crisper plate in each of the two baskets. Place a piece of parchment paper or aluminum foil over the plate in the Zone 1 basket. Place the fish in the basket and insert the basket in the unit. Place the potato wedges in a single layer in the Zone 2 basket and insert the basket in the unit.
7. Select Zone 1, select AIR FRY, set the temperature to 400°F, and set the timer to 13 minutes.
8. Select Zone 2, select AIR FRY, set the temperature to 400°F, and set the timer to 30 minutes. Select SMART FINISH.
9. Press START/PAUSE to begin cooking.
10. When the Zone 1 timer reads 5 minutes, press START/PAUSE. Remove the basket and use a silicone spatula to carefully flip the fish over. Reinsert the basket and press START/PAUSE to resume cooking.
11. When cooking is complete, the fish should be cooked through and the potatoes crispy outside and tender inside. Serve hot with tartar sauce, cocktail sauce, or malt vinegar (if using).

Nutrition:
- (Per serving) Calories: 360; Total fat: 8g; Saturated fat: 1g; Carbohydrates: 40g; Fiber: 2g; Protein: 30g; Sodium: 302mg

Italian Baked Cod

Servings: 4
Cooking Time: 12 Minutes
Ingredients:
- 4 cod fillets, 170 g each
- 2 tablespoons salted butter, melted
- 1 teaspoon Italian seasoning
- ¼ teaspoon salt
- 120 ml tomato-based pasta sauce

Directions:
1. Place cod into an ungreased round nonstick baking dish. Pour butter over cod and sprinkle with Italian seasoning and salt. Top with pasta sauce.
2. Place dish into the two air fryer drawers. Adjust the temperature to 176°C and bake for 12 minutes. Fillets will be lightly browned, easily flake, and have an internal temperature of at least 64°C when done. Serve warm.

Cod With Jalapeño

Servings: 4
Cooking Time: 14 Minutes
Ingredients:
- 4 cod fillets, boneless
- 1 jalapeño, minced
- 1 tablespoon avocado oil
- ½ teaspoon minced garlic

Directions:
1. In the shallow bowl, mix minced jalapeño, avocado oil, and minced garlic.
2. Put the cod fillets in the two air fryer drawers in one layer and top with minced jalapeño mixture.
3. Cook the fish at 185°C for 7 minutes per side.

Chili Lime Tilapia

Servings: 4
Cooking Time: 10 Minutes
Ingredients:
- 340g tilapia fillets
- 2 teaspoons chili powder
- 1 teaspoon cumin
- 1 teaspoon garlic powder
- ½ teaspoon oregano
- ½ teaspoon sea salt
- ¼ teaspoon black pepper
- Lime zest from 1 lime
- Juice of ½ lime

Directions:
1. Mix chili powder and other spices with lime juice and zest in a bowl.
2. Rub this spice mixture over the tilapia fillets.
3. Place two fillets in each air basket.
4. Return the air fryer basket to the Instant 2 Baskets Air Fryer.
5. Choose the "Air Fry" mode for Zone 1 at 400 degrees F and 10 minutes of cooking time.
6. Select the "MATCH COOK" option to copy the settings for Zone 2.
7. Initiate cooking by pressing the START/PAUSE BUTTON.
8. Flip the tilapia fillets once cooked halfway through.
9. Serve warm.

Nutrition:
- (Per serving) Calories 275 | Fat 1.4g |Sodium 582mg | Carbs 31.5g | Fiber 1.1g | Sugar 0.1g | Protein 29.8g

Marinated Ginger Garlic Salmon

Servings: 2
Cooking Time:10 Minutes
Ingredients:
- 2 salmon fillets, skinless & boneless
- 1 1/2 tbsp mirin
- 1 1/2 tbsp soy sauce
- 1 tbsp olive oil
- 2 tbsp green onion, minced
- 1 tbsp ginger, grated
- 1 tsp garlic, minced

Directions:
1. Add mirin, soy sauce, oil, green onion, ginger, and garlic into the zip-lock bag and mix well.
2. Add fish fillets into the bag, seal the bag, and place in the refrigerator for 30 minutes.
3. Preheat the air fryer to 360 F.
4. Spray air fryer basket with cooking spray.
5. Place marinated salmon fillets into the air fryer basket and cook for 10 minutes.
6. Serve and enjoy.

Bang Bang Shrimp With Roasted Bok Choy

Servings: 4
Cooking Time: 13 Minutes
Ingredients:
- FOR THE BANG BANG SHRIMP
- ½ cup all-purpose flour
- 2 large eggs
- 1 cup panko bread crumbs
- 1 pound peeled shrimp (tails removed), thawed if frozen
- Nonstick cooking spray
- ½ cup mayonnaise
- ¼ cup Thai sweet chili sauce
- ¼ teaspoon sriracha
- FOR THE BOK CHOY
- 1 tablespoon reduced-sodium soy sauce
- 1 teaspoon minced garlic
- 1 teaspoon sesame oil
- 1 teaspoon minced fresh ginger
- 1½ pounds baby bok choy, halved lengthwise
- 1 tablespoon toasted sesame seeds

Directions:
1. To prep the shrimp: Set up a breading station with three small shallow bowls. Place the flour in the first bowl. In the second bowl, whisk the eggs. Place the panko in the third bowl.
2. Bread the shrimp in this order: First, dip them into the flour, coating both sides. Then, dip into the beaten egg. Finally, coat them in the panko, gently pressing the bread crumbs to adhere to the shrimp. Spritz both sides of the shrimp with cooking spray.
3. To prep the bok choy: In a small bowl, whisk together the soy sauce, garlic, sesame oil, and ginger.
4. To cook the shrimp and bok choy: Install a crisper plate in the Zone 1 basket. Place the shrimp in the basket in a single layer and insert the basket in the unit. Place the boy choy cut-side up in the Zone 2 basket. Pour the sauce over the bok choy and insert the basket in the unit.
5. Select Zone 1, select AIR FRY, set the temperature to 390°F, and set the timer to 13 minutes.
6. Select Zone 2, select BAKE, set the temperature to 370°F, and set the timer to 8 minutes. Select SMART FINISH.
7. Press START/PAUSE to begin cooking.
8. When cooking is complete, the shrimp should be cooked through and golden brown and the bok choy soft and slightly caramelized.
9. In a large bowl, whisk together the mayonnaise, sweet chili sauce, and sriracha. Add the shrimp and toss to coat.
10. Sprinkle the bok choy with the sesame seeds and serve hot alongside the shrimp.

Nutrition:
- (Per serving) Calories: 534; Total fat: 33g; Saturated fat: 4g; Carbohydrates: 29g; Fiber: 3g; Protein: 31g; Sodium: 789mg

Cajun Scallops

Servings: 6
Cooking Time: 6 Minutes
Ingredients:
- 6 sea scallops
- Cooking spray
- Salt to taste
- Cajun seasoning

Directions:
1. Season the scallops with Cajun seasoning and salt.
2. Place them in one air fryer basket and spray them with cooking oil.
3. Return the air fryer basket 1 to Zone 1 of the Instant 2-Basket Air Fryer.
4. Choose the "Air Fry" mode for Zone 1 and set the temperature to 400 degrees F and 6 minutes of cooking time.
5. Initiate cooking by pressing the START/PAUSE BUTTON.
6. Flip the scallops once cooked halfway through.
7. Serve warm.

Nutrition:
- (Per serving) Calories 266 | Fat 6.3g |Sodium 193mg | Carbs 39.1g | Fiber 7.2g | Sugar 5.2g | Protein 14.8g

Fish Tacos

Servings: 5
Cooking Time: 30 Minutes
Ingredients:
- 1 pound firm white fish such as cod, haddock, pollock, halibut, or walleye
- ¾ cup gluten-free flour blend
- 3 eggs
- 1 cup gluten-free panko breadcrumbs
- 1 teaspoon garlic powder
- 1 teaspoon onion powder
- 1 teaspoon cumin
- 1 teaspoon lemon pepper
- 1 teaspoon red chili flakes
- 1 teaspoon kosher salt, divided
- 1 teaspoon pepper, divided
- Cooking oil spray
- 1 package corn tortillas
- Toppings such as tomatoes, avocado, cabbage, radishes, jalapenos, salsa, or hot sauce (optional)

Directions:
1. Dry the fish with paper towels. (Make sure to thaw the fish if it's frozen.) Depending on the size of the fillets, cut the fish in half or thirds.
2. On both sides of the fish pieces, liberally season with salt and pepper.
3. Put the flour in a dish.
4. In a separate bowl, crack the eggs and whisk them together until well blended.
5. Put the panko breadcrumbs in another bowl. Add the garlic powder, onion powder, cumin, lemon pepper, and red chili flakes. Add salt and pepper to taste. Stir until everything is well blended.
6. Each piece of fish should be dipped in the flour, then the eggs, and finally in the breadcrumb mixture. Make sure that each piece is completely coated.
7. Put a crisper plate in each drawer. Arrange the fish pieces in a single layer in each drawer. Insert the drawers into the unit.
8. Select zone 1, then AIR FRY, then set the temperature to 360 degrees F/ 180 degrees C with a 20-minute timer. To match zone 2 settings to zone 1, choose MATCH. To begin, select START/STOP.
9. Remove the fish from the drawers after the timer has finished. Place the crispy fish on warmed tortillas.

Nutrition:
- (Per serving) Calories 534 | Fat 18g | Sodium 679mg | Carbs 63g | Fiber 8g | Sugar 3g | Protein 27g

Tilapia Sandwiches With Tartar Sauce

Servings: 4
Cooking Time: 17 Minutes
Ingredients:
- 160 g mayonnaise
- 2 tablespoons dried minced onion
- 1 dill pickle spear, finely chopped
- 2 teaspoons pickle juice
- ¼ teaspoon salt
- ⅛ teaspoon freshly ground black pepper
- 40 g plain flour
- 1 egg, lightly beaten
- 200 g panko bread crumbs
- 2 teaspoons lemon pepper
- 4 (170 g) tilapia fillets
- Olive oil spray
- 4 soft sub rolls
- 4 lettuce leaves

Directions:
1. To make the tartar sauce, in a small bowl, whisk the mayonnaise, dried onion, pickle, pickle juice, salt, and pepper until blended. Refrigerate while you make the fish.
2. Scoop the flour onto a plate; set aside.
3. Put the beaten egg in a medium shallow bowl.
4. On another plate, stir together the panko and lemon pepper.
5. Preheat the air fryer to 205ºC.
6. Dredge the tilapia fillets in the flour, in the egg, and press into the panko mixture to coat.
7. Once the unit is preheated, spray the zone 1 basket with olive oil and place a baking paper liner into the basket. Place the prepared fillets on the liner in a single layer. Lightly spray the fillets with olive oil.
8. cook for 8 minutes, remove the basket, carefully flip the fillets, and spray them with more olive oil. Reinsert the basket to resume cooking.
9. When the cooking is complete, the fillets should be golden and crispy and a food thermometer should register 65ºC. Place each cooked fillet in a sub roll, top with a little bit of tartar sauce and lettuce, and serve.

Steamed Cod With Garlic And Swiss Chard

Servings: 4
Cooking Time: 12 Minutes
Ingredients:
- 1 teaspoon salt
- ½ teaspoon dried oregano
- ½ teaspoon dried thyme
- ½ teaspoon garlic powder
- 4 cod fillets
- ½ white onion, thinly sliced
- 135 g Swiss chard, washed, stemmed, and torn into pieces
- 60 ml olive oil
- 1 lemon, quartered

Directions:
1. Preheat the air fryer to 192ºC.
2. In a small bowl, whisk together the salt, oregano, thyme, and garlic powder.
3. Tear off four pieces of aluminum foil, with each sheet being large enough to envelop one cod fillet and a quarter of the vegetables.
4. Place a cod fillet in the middle of each sheet of foil, then sprinkle on all sides with the spice mixture.
5. In each foil packet, place a quarter of the onion slices and 30 g Swiss chard, then drizzle 1 tablespoon olive oil and squeeze ¼ lemon over the contents of each foil packet.
6. Fold and seal the sides of the foil packets and then place them into the two air fryer drawers. Steam for 12 minutes.
7. Remove from the drawers, and carefully open each packet to avoid a steam burn.

Parmesan Mackerel With Coriander And Garlic Butter Prawns Scampi

Servings: 6
Cooking Time: 8 Minutes
Ingredients:
- Parmesan Mackerel with Coriander:
- 340 g mackerel fillet
- 60 g Parmesan, grated
- 1 teaspoon ground coriander
- 1 tablespoon olive oil
- Garlic Butter Prawns Scampi:
- Sauce:
- 60 g unsalted butter
- 2 tablespoons fish stock or chicken broth
- 2 cloves garlic, minced
- 2 tablespoons chopped fresh basil leaves
- 1 tablespoon lemon juice
- 1 tablespoon chopped fresh parsley, plus more for garnish
- 1 teaspoon red pepper flakes
- Prawns:
- 455 g large prawns, peeled and deveined, tails removed
- Fresh basil sprigs, for garnish

Directions:
1. Make the Parmesan Mackerel with Coriander :
2. Sprinkle the mackerel fillet with olive oil and put it in the zone 1 air fryer drawer.
3. Top the fish with ground coriander and Parmesan.
4. Cook the fish at 200ºC for 7 minutes.
5. Make the Garlic Butter Prawns Scampi :
6. Preheat the zone 2 air fryer drawer to 176ºC.
7. Put all the ingredients for the sauce in a baking pan and stir to incorporate.
8. Transfer the baking pan to the zone 2 air fryer drawer and air fry for 3 minutes, or until the sauce is heated through.
9. Once done, add the prawns to the baking pan, flipping to coat in the sauce.
10. Return to the air fryer and cook for another 5 minutes, or until the prawns are pink and opaque. Stir the prawns twice during cooking.
11. Serve garnished with the parsley and basil sprigs.

Flavorful Salmon Fillets

Servings: 2
Cooking Time: 10 Minutes
Ingredients:
- 2 salmon fillets, boneless
- 1/2 tsp garlic powder
- 1/2 tsp ground cumin
- 1/2 tsp chili powder
- 2 tbsp fresh lemon juice
- 2 tbsp olive oil
- Pepper
- Salt

Directions:
1. In a small bowl, mix oil, lemon juice, chili powder, ground cumin, garlic powder, pepper, and salt.
2. Brush salmon fillets with oil mixture and place into the air fryer basket and cook at 400 F for 10 minutes.
3. Serve and enjoy.

Prawn Dejonghe Skewers

Servings: 4
Cooking Time: 15 Minutes
Ingredients:
- 2 teaspoons sherry, or apple cider vinegar
- 3 tablespoons unsalted butter, melted
- 120 g panko bread crumbs
- 3 cloves garlic, minced
- 8 g minced flat-leaf parsley, plus more for garnish
- 1 teaspoon kosher salt
- Pinch of cayenne pepper
- 680 g prawns, peeled and deveined
- Vegetable oil, for spraying
- Lemon wedges, for serving

Directions:
1. Stir the sherry and melted butter together in a shallow bowl or pie plate and whisk until combined. Set aside. Whisk together the panko, garlic, parsley, salt, and cayenne pepper on a large plate or shallow bowl.
2. Thread the prawns onto metal skewers designed for the air fryer or bamboo skewers, 3 to 4 per skewer. Dip 1 prawns skewer in the butter mixture, then dredge in the panko mixture until each prawns is lightly coated. Place the skewer on a plate or rimmed baking sheet and repeat the process with the remaining skewers.
3. Preheat the air fryer to 175°C. Arrange 4 skewers in the zone 1 air fryer basket. Spray the skewers with oil and air fry for 8 minutes, until the bread crumbs are golden brown and the prawns are cooked through. Transfer the cooked skewers to a serving plate and keep warm while cooking the remaining 4 skewers in the air fryer.
4. Sprinkle the cooked skewers with additional fresh parsley and serve with lemon wedges if desired.

Scallops

Servings: 4
Cooking Time: 5 Minutes
Ingredients:
- ½ cup Italian breadcrumbs
- ½ teaspoon garlic powder
- ¼ teaspoon salt
- ½ teaspoon black pepper
- 2 tablespoons butter, melted
- 1 pound sea scallops, rinsed and pat dry

Directions:
1. Combine the breadcrumbs, garlic powder, salt, and pepper in a small bowl. Pour the melted butter into another shallow bowl.
2. Dredge each scallop in the melted butter, then roll it in the breadcrumb mixture until well covered.
3. Place a crisper plate in each drawer. Put the scallops in a single layer in each drawer. Insert the drawers into the unit.
4. Select zone 1, then AIR FRY, then set the temperature to 360 degrees F/ 180 degrees C with a 5-minute timer. To match zone 2 settings to zone 1, choose MATCH. To begin, select START/STOP.
5. Press START/STOP to pause the unit when the timer reaches 3 minutes. Remove the drawers. Use tongs to carefully flip the scallops over. To resume cooking, re-insert the drawers into the unit and press START/STOP.
6. Remove the scallops from the drawers after the timer has finished.

Nutrition:
- (Per serving) Calories 81 | Fat 6g | Sodium 145mg | Carbs 3g | Fiber 4g | Sugar 1g | Protein 3g

Fried Prawns

Servings: 4
Cooking Time: 5 Minutes
Ingredients:
- 70 g self-raising flour
- 1 teaspoon paprika
- 1 teaspoon salt
- ½ teaspoon freshly ground black pepper
- 1 large egg, beaten
- 120 g finely crushed panko bread crumbs
- 20 frozen large prawns (about 900 g), peeled and deveined
- Cooking spray

Directions:
1. In a shallow bowl, whisk the flour, paprika, salt, and pepper until blended. Add the beaten egg to a second shallow bowl and the bread crumbs to a third.
2. One at a time, dip the prawns into the flour, the egg, and the bread crumbs, coating thoroughly.
3. Preheat the air fryer to 205°C. Line the two air fryer baskets with baking paper.
4. Place the prawns on the baking paper and spritz with oil.
5. Air fry for 2 minutes. Shake the baskets, spritz the prawns with oil, and air fry for 3 minutes more until lightly browned and crispy. Serve hot.

Garlic Shrimp With Pasta Alfredo

Servings: 4
Cooking Time: 40 Minutes
Ingredients:
- FOR THE GARLIC SHRIMP
- 1 pound peeled small shrimp, thawed if frozen
- 1 tablespoon olive oil
- 1 tablespoon minced garlic
- ¼ teaspoon sea salt
- ¼ cup chopped fresh parsley
- FOR THE PASTA ALFREDO
- 8 ounces no-boil lasagna noodles
- 2 cups whole milk
- ¼ cup heavy (whipping) cream
- 2 tablespoons unsalted butter, cut into small pieces
- 1 tablespoon minced garlic
- ½ teaspoon kosher salt
- ¼ teaspoon freshly ground black pepper
- ½ cup grated Parmesan cheese

Directions:
1. To prep the garlic shrimp: In a large bowl, combine the shrimp, oil, garlic, and salt.
2. To prep the pasta alfredo: Break the lasagna noodles into 2-inch pieces. Add the milk to the Zone 2 basket, then add the noodles, cream, butter, garlic, salt, and black pepper. Stir well and ensure the pasta is fully submerged in the liquid.
3. To cook the shrimp and pasta: Install a crisper plate in the Zone 1 basket. Place the shrimp in the basket and insert the basket in the unit. Insert the Zone 2 basket in the unit.
4. Select Zone 1, select AIR FRY, set the temperature to 390°F, and set the timer to 13 minutes.
5. Select Zone 2, select BAKE, set the temperature to 360°F, and set the timer to 40 minutes. Select SMART FINISH.
6. Press START/PAUSE to begin cooking.
7. When the Zone 2 timer reads 20 minutes, press START/PAUSE. Remove the basket and stir the pasta. Reinsert the basket and press START/PAUSE to resume cooking.
8. When cooking is complete, the shrimp will be cooked through and the pasta tender.
9. Transfer the pasta to a serving dish and stir in the Parmesan. Top with the shrimp and parsley.

Nutrition:
- (Per serving) Calories: 542; Total fat: 23g; Saturated fat: 11g; Carbohydrates: 52g; Fiber: 2g; Protein: 34g; Sodium: 643mg

Fried Lobster Tails

Servings: 4
Cooking Time: 18 Minutes
Ingredients:
- 4 (4-oz) lobster tails
- 8 tablespoons butter, melted
- 2 teaspoons lemon zest
- 2 garlic cloves, grated
- Salt and black pepper, ground to taste
- 2 teaspoons fresh parsley, chopped
- 4 wedges lemon

Directions:
1. Spread the lobster tails into Butterfly, slit the top to expose the lobster meat while keeping the tail intact.
2. Place two lobster tails in each of the crisper plate with their lobster meat facing up.
3. Mix melted butter with lemon zest and garlic in a bowl.
4. Brush the butter mixture on top of the lobster tails.
5. And drizzle salt and black pepper on top.
6. Return the crisper plate to the Instant Dual Zone Air Fryer.
7. Choose the Air Fry mode for Zone 1 and set the temperature to 390 degrees F and the time to 18 minutes|
8. Select the "MATCH" button to copy the settings for Zone 2.
9. Initiate cooking by pressing the START/STOP button.
10. Garnish with parsley and lemon wedges.
11. Serve warm.

Classic Fish Sticks With Tartar Sauce

Servings: 4
Cooking Time: 12 To 15 Minutes
Ingredients:
- 680 g cod fillets, cut into 1-inch strips
- 1 teaspoon salt
- ½ teaspoon freshly ground black pepper
- 2 eggs
- 70 g almond flour
- 20 g grated Parmesan cheese
- Tartar Sauce:
- 120 ml sour cream
- 120 ml mayonnaise
- 3 tablespoons chopped dill pickle
- 2 tablespoons capers, drained and chopped
- ½ teaspoon dried dill
- 1 tablespoon dill pickle liquid (optional)

Directions:
1. Preheat the air fryer to 204°C. 2. Season the cod with the salt and black pepper; set aside. 3. In a shallow bowl, lightly beat the eggs. In a second shallow bowl, combine the almond flour and Parmesan cheese. Stir until thoroughly combined. 4. Working with a few pieces at a time, dip the fish into the egg mixture followed by the flour mixture. Press lightly to ensure an even coating. 5. Arrange the fish in a single layer in the two air fryer drawers and spray lightly with olive oil. Pausing halfway through the cooking time to turn the fish, air fry for 12 to 15 minutes, until the fish flakes easily with a fork. Let sit in the drawer for a few minutes before serving with the tartar sauce. 6. To make the tartar sauce: In a small bowl, combine the sour cream, mayonnaise, pickle, capers, and dill. If you prefer a thinner sauce, stir in the pickle liquid.

Tuna Patties

Servings: 6
Cooking Time: 10 Minutes
Ingredients:
- For the tuna patties:
- 1 tablespoon extra-virgin olive oil
- 1 tablespoon butter
- ½ cup chopped onion
- ½ red bell pepper, chopped
- 1 teaspoon minced garlic
- 2 (7-ounce) cans or 3 (5-ounce) cans albacore tuna fish in water, drained
- 1 tablespoon lime juice
- 1 celery stalk, chopped
- ¼ cup chopped fresh parsley
- 3 tablespoons grated parmesan cheese
- ½ teaspoon dried oregano
- ¼ teaspoon salt
- Black pepper, to taste
- 1 teaspoon sriracha
- ½ cup panko crumbs
- 2 whisked eggs
- For the crumb coating:
- ½ cup panko crumbs
- ¼ cup parmesan cheese
- Non-stick spray

Directions:
1. In a skillet, heat the oil and butter over medium-high heat.
2. Sauté the onions, red bell pepper, and garlic for 5 to 7 minutes.
3. Drain the tuna from the cans thoroughly. Put the tuna in a large mixing bowl. Add the lime juice.
4. Add the sautéed vegetables to the mixing bowl.
5. Add the celery, parsley, and cheese. Combine well.
6. Add the oregano, salt, and pepper to taste. Mix well.
7. Add a dash of sriracha for a spicy kick and mix well.
8. Add the panko crumbs and mix well.
9. Mix in the eggs until the mixture is well combined. You can add an extra egg if necessary, but the tuna is usually wet enough that it isn't required. Form 6 patties from the mixture.
10. Refrigerate for 30 to 60 minutes (or even overnight).
11. Remove from refrigerator and coat with a mixture of the ½ cup of panko crumbs and ¼ cup of parmesan cheese.
12. Spray the tops of the coated patties with some non-stick cooking spray.
13. Place a crisper place in each drawer. Put 3 patties in each drawer. Insert the drawers into the unit.
14. Select zone 1, then AIR FRY, then set the temperature to 390 degrees F/ 200 degrees C with a 10-minute timer. To match zone 2 settings to zone 1, choose MATCH. To begin, select START/STOP.
15. Remove and garnish with chopped parsley.

Nutrition:
- (Per serving) Calories 381 | Fat 16g | Sodium 1007mg | Carbs 23g | Fiber 2g | Sugar 4g | Protein 38g

Two-way Salmon

Servings: 2
Cooking Time: 18
Ingredients:
- 2 salmon fillets, 8 ounces each
- 2 tablespoons of Cajun seasoning
- 2 tablespoons of jerk seasoning
- 1 lemon cut in half
- oil spray, for greasing

Directions:
1. First, drizzle lemon juice over the salmon and wash it with tap water.
2. Rinse and pat dry the fillets with a paper towel.
3. Now rub o fillet with Cajun seasoning and grease it with oil spray.
4. Take the second fillet and rub it with jerk seasoning.
5. Grease the second fillet of salmon with oil spray.
6. now put the salmon fillets in both the baskets.
7. Set the Zone 1 basket to 390 degrees F for 16-18 minutes
8. Select MATCH button for zone 2 basket.
9. hit the start button to start cooking.
10. Once the cooking is done, serve the fish hot with mayonnaise.

Nutrition:
- (Per serving) Calories 238| Fat 11.8g| Sodium 488mg | Carbs 9g | Fiber 0g | Sugar8 g | Protein 35g

Lemon-pepper Trout

Servings: 4
Cooking Time: 15 Minutes
Ingredients:
- 4 trout fillets
- 2 tablespoons olive oil
- ½ teaspoon salt
- 1 teaspoon black pepper
- 2 garlic cloves, sliced
- 1 lemon, sliced, plus additional wedges for serving

Directions:
1. Preheat the air fryer to 190ºC.
2. Brush each fillet with olive oil on both sides and season with salt and pepper. Place the fillets in an even layer in the two air fryer baskets.
3. Place the sliced garlic over the tops of the trout fillets, then top the garlic with lemon slices and roast for 12 to 15 minutes, or until it has reached an internal temperature of 65ºC.
4. Serve with fresh lemon wedges.

Garlic Butter Prawns Scampi & Coconut Prawns

Servings: 6
Cooking Time: 8 Minutes
Ingredients:
- Garlic Butter Prawns Scampi:
- Sauce:
- 60 g unsalted butter
- 2 tablespoons fish stock or chicken broth
- 2 cloves garlic, minced
- 2 tablespoons chopped fresh basil leaves
- 1 tablespoon lemon juice
- 1 tablespoon chopped fresh parsley, plus more for garnish
- 1 teaspoon red pepper flakes
- Prawns:
- 455 g large prawns, peeled and deveined, tails removed
- Fresh basil sprigs, for garnish
- Coconut Prawns:
- 230 g medium prawns, peeled and deveined
- 2 tablespoons salted butter, melted
- ½ teaspoon Old Bay seasoning
- 25 g desiccated, unsweetened coconut

Directions:
1. Make the Garlic Butter Prawns Scampi :
2. Preheat the air fryer to 175ºC.
3. Put all the ingredients for the sauce in a baking pan and stir to incorporate.
4. Transfer the baking pan to the zone 1 air fryer basket and air fry for 3 minutes, or until the sauce is heated through.
5. Once done, add the prawns to the baking pan, flipping to coat in the sauce.
6. Return to the air fryer and cook for another 5 minutes, or until the prawns are pink and opaque. Stir the prawns twice during cooking.
7. Serve garnished with the parsley and basil sprigs.
8. Make the Coconut Prawns :
9. In a large bowl, toss the prawns in butter and Old Bay seasoning.
10. Place shredded coconut in bowl. Coat each piece of prawns in the coconut and place into the zone 2 air fryer basket.
11. Adjust the temperature to 205ºC and air fry for 6 minutes.
12. Gently turn the prawns halfway through the cooking time. Serve immediately.

Smoked Salmon

Servings: 4
Cooking Time: 12
Ingredients:
- 2 pounds of salmon fillets, smoked
- 6 ounces cream cheese
- 4 tablespoons mayonnaise
- 2 teaspoons of chives, fresh
- 1 teaspoon of lemon zest
- Salt and freshly ground black pepper, to taste
- 2 tablespoons of butter

Directions:
1. Cut the salmon into very small and uniform bite-size pieces.
2. Mix cream cheese, chives, mayonnaise, black pepper, and lemon zest, in a small mixing bowl.
3. Let it sit aside for further use.
4. Coat the salmon pieces with salt and butter.
5. Divide the bite-size pieces into both zones of the air fryer.
6. Set it on AIRFRY mode at 400 degrees F for 12 minutes.
7. Select MATCH for zone 2 basket.
8. Hit start, so the cooking start.
9. Once the salmon is done, top it with a bowl creamy mixture and serve.
10. Enjoy hot.

Nutrition:
- (Per serving) Calories 557| Fat 15.7 g| Sodium 371mg | Carbs 4.8 g | Fiber 0g | Sugar 1.1g | Protein 48 g

Basil Cheese S·saltalmon

Servings: 4
Cooking Time: 7 Minutes
Ingredients:
- 4 salmon fillets
- 1/4 cup parmesan cheese, grated
- 5 fresh basil leaves, minced
- 2 tbsp mayonnaise
- 1/2 lemon juice
- Pepper

Directions:
1. Preheat the air fryer to 400 F.
2. Brush salmon fillets with lemon juice and season with pepper and salt.
3. In a small bowl, mix mayonnaise, basil, and cheese.
4. Spray air fryer basket with cooking spray.
5. Place salmon fillets into the air fryer basket and brush with mayonnaise mixture and cook for 7 minutes.
6. Serve and enjoy.

Cajun Catfish Cakes With Cheese

Servings: 4
Cooking Time: 35 Minutes
Ingredients:
- 2 catfish fillets
- 85 g butter
- 150 g shredded Parmesan cheese
- 150 g shredded Swiss cheese
- 120 ml buttermilk
- 1 teaspoon baking powder
- 1 teaspoon baking soda
- 1 teaspoon Cajun seasoning

Directions:
1. Bring a pot of salted water to a boil. Add the catfish fillets to the boiling water and let them boil for 5 minutes until they become opaque.
2. Remove the fillets from the pot to a mixing bowl and flake them into small pieces with a fork.
3. Add the remaining ingredients to the bowl of fish and stir until well incorporated.
4. Divide the fish mixture into 12 equal portions and shape each portion into a patty.
5. Preheat the air fryer to 190°C.
6. Arrange the patties in the two air fryer baskets and air fry for 15 minutes until golden brown and cooked through. Flip the patties halfway through the cooking time.
7. Let the patties sit for 5 minutes and serve.

Parmesan Fish Fillets

Servings: 4
Cooking Time: 17 Minutes
Ingredients:
- 50 g grated Parmesan cheese
- ½ teaspoon fennel seed
- ½ teaspoon tarragon
- ⅓ teaspoon mixed peppercorns
- 2 eggs, beaten
- 4 (110 g) fish fillets, halved
- 2 tablespoons dry white wine
- 1 teaspoon seasoned salt

Directions:
1. Preheat the air fryer to 175°C.
2. Place the grated Parmesan cheese, fennel seed, tarragon, and mixed peppercorns in a food processor and pulse for about 20 seconds until well combined. Transfer the cheese mixture to a shallow dish.
3. Place the beaten eggs in another shallow dish.
4. Drizzle the dry white wine over the top of fish fillets. Dredge each fillet in the beaten eggs on both sides, shaking off any excess, then roll them in the cheese mixture until fully coated. Season with the salt.
5. Arrange the fillets in the two air fryer baskets and air fry for about 17 minutes, or until the fish is cooked through and no longer translucent. Flip the fillets once halfway through the cooking time.
6. Cool for 5 minutes before serving.

Scallops And Spinach With Cream Sauce And Confetti Salmon Burgers

Servings: 6
Cooking Time: 12 Minutes
Ingredients:
- Scallops and Spinach with Cream Sauce:
- Vegetable oil spray
- 280 g frozen spinach, thawed and drained
- 8 jumbo sea scallops
- Kosher or coarse sea salt, and black pepper, to taste
- 180 ml heavy cream
- 1 tablespoon tomato paste
- 1 tablespoon chopped fresh basil
- 1 teaspoon minced garlic
- Confetti Salmon Burgers:
- 400 g cooked fresh or canned salmon, flaked with a fork
- 40 g minced spring onions, white and light green parts only
- 40 g minced red bell pepper
- 40 g minced celery
- 2 small lemons
- 1 teaspoon crab boil seasoning such as Old Bay
- ½ teaspoon kosher or coarse sea salt
- ½ teaspoon black pepper
- 1 egg, beaten
- 30 g fresh bread crumbs
- Vegetable oil, for spraying

Directions:
1. Make the Scallops and Spinach with Cream Sauce :
2. Spray a baking pan with vegetable oil spray. Spread the thawed spinach in an even layer in the bottom of the pan.
3. Spray both sides of the scallops with vegetable oil spray. Season lightly with salt and pepper. Arrange the scallops on top of the spinach.
4. In a small bowl, whisk together the cream, tomato paste, basil, garlic, ½ teaspoon salt, and ½ teaspoon pepper. Pour the sauce over the scallops and spinach.
5. Place the pan in the zone 1 air fryer drawer. Set the temperature to 176°C for 10 minutes. Use a meat thermometer to ensure the scallops have an internal temperature of 56°C.
6. Make the Confetti Salmon Burgers :
7. In a large bowl, combine the salmon, vegetables, the zest and juice of 1 of the lemons, crab boil seasoning, salt, and pepper. Add the egg and bread crumbs and stir to combine. Form the mixture into 4 patties weighing approximately 140 g each. Chill until firm, about 15 minutes.
8. Preheat the 2 air fryer drawer to 204°C.
9. Spray the salmon patties with oil on all sides and spray the zone 2 air fryer drawer to prevent sticking. Air fry for 12 minutes, flipping halfway through, until the burgers are browned and cooked through. Cut the remaining lemon into 4 wedges and serve with the burgers.

Snapper Scampi

Servings: 4
Cooking Time: 8 To 10 Minutes
Ingredients:
- 4 skinless snapper or arctic char fillets, 170 g each
- 1 tablespoon olive oil
- 3 tablespoons lemon juice, divided
- ½ teaspoon dried basil
- Pinch salt
- Freshly ground black pepper, to taste
- 2 tablespoons butter
- 2 cloves garlic, minced

Directions:
1. Rub the fish fillets with olive oil and 1 tablespoon of the lemon juice. Sprinkle with the basil, salt, and pepper, and place in the two air fryer drawers.
2. Air fry the fish at 192°C for 7 to 8 minutes or until the fish just flakes when tested with a fork. Remove the fish from the drawers and put on a serving plate. Cover to keep warm.
3. In a baking pan, combine the butter, remaining 2 tablespoons lemon juice, and garlic. Bake in the air fryer for 1 to 2 minutes or until the garlic is sizzling. Pour this mixture over the fish and serve

Roasted Salmon Fillets & Chilli Lime Prawns

Servings: 6
Cooking Time: 10 Minutes
Ingredients:
- Roasted Salmon Fillets:
- 2 (230 g) skin-on salmon fillets, 1½ inches thick
- 1 teaspoon vegetable oil
- Salt and pepper, to taste
- Vegetable oil spray
- Chilli Lime Prawns:
- 455 g medium prawns, peeled and deveined
- 1 tablespoon salted butter, melted
- 2 teaspoons chilli powder
- ¼ teaspoon garlic powder
- ¼ teaspoon salt
- ¼ teaspoon ground black pepper
- ½ small lime, zested and juiced, divided

Directions:
1. Make the Roasted Salmon Fillets :
2. Preheat the air fryer to 205°C.
3. Make foil sling for air fryer basket by folding 1 long sheet of aluminum foil so it is 4 inches wide. Lay sheet of foil widthwise across zone 1 basket, pressing foil into and up sides of basket. Fold excess foil as needed so that edges of foil are flush with top of basket. Lightly spray foil and basket with vegetable oil spray.
4. Pat salmon dry with paper towels, rub with oil, and season with salt and pepper. Arrange fillets skin side down on sling in prepared zone 1 basket, spaced evenly apart. Air fry salmon until center is still translucent when checked with the tip of a paring knife and registers 50°C , 10 to 14 minutes, using sling to rotate fillets halfway through cooking.
5. Using the sling, carefully remove salmon from air fryer. Slide fish spatula along underside of fillets and transfer to individual serving plates, leaving skin behind. Serve.
6. Make the Chilli Lime Prawns :
7. In a medium bowl, toss prawns with butter, then sprinkle with chilli powder, garlic powder, salt, pepper, and lime zest.
8. Place prawns into ungreased zone 2 air fryer basket. Adjust the temperature to 205°C and air fry for 5 minutes. Prawns will be firm and form a "C" shape when done.
9. Transfer prawns to a large serving dish and drizzle with lime juice. Serve warm.

Furikake Salmon

Servings: 4
Cooking Time: 10 Minutes
Ingredients:
- ½ cup mayonnaise
- 1 tablespoon shoyu
- 455g salmon fillet
- Salt and black pepper to taste
- 2 tablespoons furikake

Directions:
1. Mix shoyu with mayonnaise in a small bowl.
2. Rub the salmon with black pepper and salt.
3. Place the salmon pieces in the air fryer baskets.
4. Top them with the mayo mixture.
5. Return the air fryer basket 1 to Zone 1, and basket 2 to Zone 2 of the Instant 2-Basket Air Fryer.
6. Choose the "Air Fry" mode for Zone 1 at 400 degrees F and 10 minutes of cooking time.
7. Select the "MATCH COOK" option to copy the settings for Zone 2.
8. Initiate cooking by pressing the START/PAUSE BUTTON.
9. Serve warm.

Nutrition:
- (Per serving) Calories 297 | Fat 1g |Sodium 291mg | Carbs 35g | Fiber 1g | Sugar 9g | Protein 29g

Tuna With Herbs

Servings: 4
Cooking Time: 17 Minutes
Ingredients:
- 1 tablespoon butter, melted
- 1 medium-sized leek, thinly sliced
- 1 tablespoon chicken stock
- 1 tablespoon dry white wine
- 455 g tuna
- ½ teaspoon red pepper flakes, crushed
- Sea salt and ground black pepper, to taste
- ½ teaspoon dried rosemary
- ½ teaspoon dried basil
- ½ teaspoon dried thyme
- 2 small ripe tomatoes, puréed
- 120 g Parmesan cheese, grated

Directions:
1. Melt ½ tablespoon of butter in a sauté pan over medium-high heat. Now, cook the leek and garlic until tender and aromatic. Add the stock and wine to deglaze the pan.
2. Preheat the air fryer to 190°C.
3. Grease a casserole dish with the remaining ½ tablespoon of melted butter. Place the fish in the casserole dish. Add the seasonings. Top with the sautéed leek mixture. Add the tomato purée. Cook for 10 minutes in the preheated air fryer. Top with grated Parmesan cheese; cook an additional 7 minutes until the crumbs are golden. Bon appétit!

Herb Lemon Mussels

Servings: 6
Cooking Time: 10 Minutes
Ingredients:
- 1kg mussels, steamed & half shell
- 1 tbsp thyme, chopped
- 1 tbsp parsley, chopped
- 1 tsp dried parsley
- 1 tsp garlic, minced
- 60ml olive oil
- 45ml lemon juice
- Pepper
- Salt

Directions:
1. In a bowl, mix mussels with the remaining ingredients.
2. Insert a crisper plate in the Instant air fryer baskets.
3. Add the mussels to both baskets.
4. Select zone 1 then select "air fry" mode and set the temperature to 360 degrees F for 10 minutes. Press "match" to match zone 2 settings to zone 1. Press "start/stop" to begin.

Nutrition:
- (Per serving) Calories 206 | Fat 11.9g |Sodium 462mg | Carbs 6.3g | Fiber 0.3g | Sugar 0.2g | Protein 18.2g

Codfish With Herb Vinaigrette

Servings:2
Cooking Time:16
Ingredients:
- Vinaigrette Ingredients:
- 1/2 cup parsley leaves
- 1 cup basil leaves
- ½ cup mint leaves
- 2 tablespoons thyme leaves
- 1/4 teaspoon red pepper flakes
- 2 cloves of garlic
- 4 tablespoons of red wine vinegar
- ¼ cup of olive oil
- Salt, to taste
- Other Ingredients:
- 1.5 pounds fish fillets, cod fish
- 2 tablespoons olive oil
- Salt and black pepper, to taste
- 1 teaspoon of paprika
- 1teasbpoon of Italian seasoning

Directions:
1. Blend the entire vinaigrette ingredient in a high-speed blender and pulse into a smooth paste.
2. Set aside for drizzling overcooked fish.
3. Rub the fillets with salt, black pepper, paprika, Italian seasoning, and olive oil.
4. Divide it between two baskets of the air fryer.
5. Set the zone 1 to 16 minutes at 390 degrees F, at AIR FRY mode.
6. Press the MATCH button for the second basket.
7. Once done, serve the fillets with the drizzle of blended vinaigrette

Nutrition:
- (Per serving) Calories 1219| Fat 81.8g| Sodium 1906mg | Carbs64.4 g | Fiber5.5 g | Sugar 0.4g | Protein 52.1g

Poultry Recipes

Buttermilk Fried Chicken

Servings: 6
Cooking Time: 30 Minutes
Ingredients:
- 1½ pounds boneless, skinless chicken thighs
- 2 cups buttermilk
- 1 cup all-purpose flour
- 1 tablespoon seasoned salt
- ½ tablespoon ground black pepper
- 1 cup panko breadcrumbs
- Cooking spray

Directions:
1. Place the chicken thighs in a shallow baking dish. Cover with the buttermilk. Refrigerate for 4 hours or overnight.
2. In a large gallon-sized resealable bag, combine the flour, seasoned salt, and pepper.
3. Remove the chicken from the buttermilk but don't discard the mixture.
4. Add the chicken to the bag and shake well to coat.
5. Dip the thighs in the buttermilk again, then coat in the panko breadcrumbs.
6. Install a crisper plate in each drawer. Place half the chicken thighs in the zone 1 drawer and half in zone 2's, then insert the drawers into the unit.
7. Select zone 1, select AIR FRY, set temperature to 390 degrees F/ 200 degrees C, and set time to 30 minutes. Select MATCH to match zone 2 settings to zone 1. Press the START/STOP button to begin cooking.
8. When the time reaches 15 minutes, press START/STOP to pause the unit. Remove the drawers and flip the chicken. Re-insert the drawers into the unit and press START/STOP to resume cooking.
9. When cooking is complete, remove the chicken.

Nutrition:
- (Per serving) Calories 335 | Fat 12.8g | Sodium 687mg | Carbs 33.1g | Fiber 0.4g | Sugar 4g | Protein 24.5g

Crispy Sesame Chicken

Servings: 2
Cooking Time: 10 Minutes
Ingredients:
- 680g boneless chicken thighs, diced
- 2 tablespoons rice vinegar
- 1 tablespoon soy sauce
- 2 teaspoons minced fresh ginger
- 1 garlic clove, minced
- ¾ teaspoon salt
- ½ teaspoon black pepper
- 2 large eggs, beaten
- 1 cup cornstarch
- Sauce
- 59ml soy sauce
- 2 tablespoons rice vinegar
- ⅓ cup brown sugar
- 59ml water
- 1 tablespoon cornstarch
- 2 teaspoons sesame oil
- 2 tablespoons vegetable oil
- 2 garlic cloves, minced
- 2 teaspoons chile paste
- Garnish
- 1 tablespoon toasted sesame seeds

Directions:
1. Blend all the sauce ingredients in a saucepan and cook until it thickens then allow it to cool.
2. Mix chicken with black pepper, salt, garlic, ginger, vinegar, and soy sauce in a bowl.
3. Cover and marinate the chicken for 20 minutes.
4. Divide the chicken in the air fryer baskets.
5. Return the air fryer basket 1 to Zone 1, and basket 2 to Zone 2 of the Instant 2-Basket Air Fryer.
6. Choose the "Air Fry" mode for Zone 1 and set the temperature to 400 degrees F and 10 minutes of cooking time.
7. Select the "MATCH COOK" option to copy the settings for Zone 2.
8. Initiate cooking by pressing the START/PAUSE BUTTON.
9. Pour the prepared sauce over the air fried chicken and drizzle sesame seeds on top.
10. Serve warm.

Nutrition:
- (Per serving) Calories 351 | Fat 16g | Sodium 777mg | Carbs 26g | Fiber 4g | Sugar 5g | Protein 28g

Buffalo Chicken

Servings: 4
Cooking Time: 22 Minutes
Ingredients:
- ½ cup plain fat-free Greek yogurt
- ¼ cup egg substitute
- 1 tablespoon plus 1 teaspoon hot sauce
- 1 cup panko breadcrumbs
- 1 tablespoon sweet paprika
- 1 tablespoon garlic pepper seasoning
- 1 tablespoon cayenne pepper
- 1-pound skinless, boneless chicken breasts, cut into 1-inch strips

Directions:
1. Combine the Greek yogurt, egg substitute, and hot sauce in a mixing bowl.
2. In a separate bowl, combine the panko breadcrumbs, paprika, garlic powder, and cayenne pepper.
3. Dip the chicken strips in the yogurt mixture, then coat them in the breadcrumb mixture.
4. Install a crisper plate in both drawers. Place the chicken strips into the drawers and then insert the drawers into the unit.
5. Select zone 1, select AIR FRY, set temperature to 390 degrees F/ 200 degrees C, and set time to 22 minutes. Select MATCH to match zone 2 settings to zone 1. Press the START/STOP button to begin cooking.
6. When cooking is complete, serve immediately.

Nutrition:
- (Per serving) Calories 234 | Fat 15.8g | Sodium 696mg | Carbs 22.1g | Fiber 1.1g | Sugar 1.7g | Protein 31.2g

Cornish Hen With Baked Potatoes

Servings: 2
Cooking Time: 45
Ingredients:
- Salt, to taste
- 1 large potato
- 1 tablespoon of avocado oil
- 1.5 pounds of Cornish hen, skinless and whole
- 2-3 teaspoons of poultry seasoning, dry rub

Directions:
1. Take a fork and pierce the large potato.
2. Rub the potato with avocado oil and salt.
3. Now put the potatoes in the first basket.
4. Now pick the Cornish hen and season the hen with poultry seasoning (dry rub) and salt.
5. Remember to coat the whole Cornish hen well.
6. Put the potato in zone 1 basket.
7. Now place the hen into zone 2 baskets.
8. Now hit 1 for the first basket and set it to AIR FRY mode at 350 degrees F, for 45 minutes.
9. For the second basket hit 2 and set the time to 45 minutes at 350 degrees F.
10. To start cooking, hit the smart finish button and press hit start.
11. Once the cooking cycle complete, turn off the air fryer and take out the potatoes and Cornish hen from both air fryer baskets.
12. Serve hot and enjoy.

Nutrition:
- (Per serving) Calories 612 | Fat 14.3 g| Sodium 304mg | Carbs 33.4 g | Fiber 4.5 g | Sugar 1.5g | Protein 83.2 g

Simply Terrific Turkey Meatballs

Servings: 4
Cooking Time: 7 To 10 Minutes
Ingredients:
- 1 red bell pepper, seeded and coarsely chopped
- 2 cloves garlic, coarsely chopped
- 15 g chopped fresh parsley
- 680 g 85% lean turkey mince
- 1 egg, lightly beaten
- 45 g grated Parmesan cheese
- 1 teaspoon salt
- ½ teaspoon freshly ground black pepper

Directions:
1. Preheat the air fryer to 200°C.
2. In a food processor fitted with a metal blade, combine the bell pepper, garlic, and parsley. Pulse until finely chopped. Transfer the vegetables to a large mixing bowl.
3. Add the turkey, egg, Parmesan, salt, and black pepper. Mix gently until thoroughly combined. Shape the mixture into 1¼-inch meatballs.
4. Arrange the meatballs in a single layer in the two air fryer drawers; coat lightly with olive oil spray. Pausing halfway through the cooking time to shake the drawer, air fry for 7 to 10 minutes, until lightly browned and a thermometer inserted into the centre of a meatball registers 76°C.

Fajita Chicken Strips & Barbecued Chicken With Creamy Coleslaw

Servings: 6
Cooking Time: 20 Minutes
Ingredients:
- Fajita Chicken Strips:
- 450 g boneless, skinless chicken tenderloins, cut into strips
- 3 bell peppers, any color, cut into chunks
- 1 onion, cut into chunks
- 1 tablespoon olive oil
- 1 tablespoon fajita seasoning mix
- Cooking spray
- Barbecued Chicken with Creamy Coleslaw:
- 270 g shredded coleslaw mix
- Salt and pepper
- 2 (340 g) bone-in split chicken breasts, trimmed
- 1 teaspoon vegetable oil
- 2 tablespoons barbecue sauce, plus extra for serving
- 2 tablespoons mayonnaise
- 2 tablespoons sour cream
- 1 teaspoon distilled white vinegar, plus extra for seasoning
- ¼ teaspoon sugar

Directions:
1. Make the Fajita Chicken Strips :
2. Preheat the air fryer to 190°C.
3. In a large bowl, mix together the chicken, bell peppers, onion, olive oil, and fajita seasoning mix until completely coated.
4. Spray the zone 1 air fryer basket lightly with cooking spray.
5. Place the chicken and vegetables in the zone 1 air fryer basket and lightly spray with cooking spray.
6. Air fry for 7 minutes. Shake the basket and air fry for an additional 5 to 8 minutes, until the chicken is cooked through and the veggies are starting to char.
7. Serve warm.
8. Make the Barbecued Chicken with Creamy Coleslaw :
9. Preheat the air fryer to 180°C.
10. Toss coleslaw mix and ¼ teaspoon salt in a colander set over bowl. Let sit until wilted slightly, about 30 minutes. Rinse, drain, and dry well with a dish towel.
11. Meanwhile, pat chicken dry with paper towels, rub with oil, and season with salt and pepper. Arrange breasts skin-side down in zone 2 air fryer basket, spaced evenly apart, alternating ends. Bake for 10 minutes. Flip breasts and brush skin side with barbecue sauce. Return basket to air fryer and bake until well browned and chicken registers 70°C, 10 to 15 minutes.
12. Transfer chicken to serving platter, tent loosely with aluminum foil, and let rest for 5 minutes. While chicken rests, whisk mayonnaise, sour cream, vinegar, sugar, and pinch pepper together in a large bowl. Stir in coleslaw mix and season with salt, pepper, and additional vinegar to taste. Serve chicken with coleslaw, passing extra barbecue sauce separately.

Cheddar-stuffed Chicken

Servings: 4
Cooking Time: 20 Minutes
Ingredients:
- 3 bacon strips, cooked and crumbled
- 2 ounces Cheddar cheese, cubed
- ¼ cup barbeque sauce
- 2 (4 ounces) boneless chicken breasts
- Salt and black pepper to taste

Directions:
1. Make a 1-inch deep pouch in each chicken breast.
2. Mix cheddar cubes with half of the BBQ sauce, salt, black pepper, and bacon.
3. Divide this filling in the chicken breasts and secure the edges with a toothpick.
4. Brush the remaining BBQ sauce over the chicken breasts.
5. Place the chicken in the crisper plate and spray them with cooking oil.
6. Return the crisper plate to the Instant Dual Zone Air Fryer.
7. Choose the Air Fry mode for Zone 1 and set the temperature to 360 degrees F and the time to 20 minutes|
8. Initiate cooking by pressing the START/STOP button.
9. Serve warm.

Lemon Chicken Thighs

Servings: 4
Cooking Time: 25 Minutes
Ingredients:
- ¼ cup butter, softened
- 3 garlic cloves, minced
- 2 teaspoons minced fresh rosemary or ½ teaspoon crushed dried rosemary
- 1 teaspoon minced fresh thyme or ¼ teaspoon dried thyme
- 1 teaspoon grated lemon zest
- 1 tablespoon lemon juice
- 4 bone-in chicken thighs (about 1½ pounds)
- ⅛ teaspoon salt
- ⅛ teaspoon pepper

Directions:
1. Combine the butter, garlic, rosemary, thyme, lemon zest, and lemon juice in a small bowl.
2. Under the skin of each chicken thigh, spread 1 teaspoon of the butter mixture. Apply the remaining butter to each thigh's skin. Season to taste with salt and pepper.
3. Install a crisper plate in both drawers. Place half the chicken tenders in the zone 1 drawer and half in zone 2's, then insert the drawers into the unit.
4. Select zone 1, select AIR FRY, set temperature to 390 degrees F/ 200 degrees C, and set time to 22 minutes. Select MATCH to match zone 2 settings to zone 1. Press the START/STOP button to begin cooking.
5. When the time reaches 11 minutes, press START/STOP to pause the unit. Remove the drawers and flip the chicken. Re-insert the drawers into the unit and press START/STOP to resume cooking.
6. When cooking is complete, remove the chicken and serve.

Nutrition:
- (Per serving) Calories 329 | Fat 26g | Sodium 253mg | Carbs 1g | Fiber 0g | Sugar 0g | Protein 23g

Curried Orange Honey Chicken

Servings: 4
Cooking Time: 16 To 19 Minutes
Ingredients:
- 340 g boneless, skinless chicken thighs, cut into 1-inch pieces
- 1 yellow bell pepper, cut into 1½-inch pieces
- 1 small red onion, sliced
- Olive oil for misting
- 60 ml chicken stock
- 2 tablespoons honey
- 60 ml orange juice
- 1 tablespoon cornflour
- 2 to 3 teaspoons curry powder

Directions:
1. Preheat the air fryer to 190°C.
2. Put the chicken thighs, pepper, and red onion in the zone 1 air fryer drawer and mist with olive oil.
3. Roast for 12 to 14 minutes or until the chicken is cooked to 76°C, shaking the drawer halfway through cooking time.
4. Remove the chicken and vegetables from the air fryer drawer and set aside.
5. In a metal bowl, combine the stock, honey, orange juice, cornflour, and curry powder, and mix well. Add the chicken and vegetables, stir, and put the bowl in the drawer.
6. Return the drawer to the air fryer and roast for 2 minutes. Remove and stir, then roast for 2 to 3 minutes or until the sauce is thickened and bubbly.
7. Serve warm.

Chicken & Veggies

Servings: 4
Cooking Time: 10 Minutes
Ingredients:
- 450g chicken breast, boneless & cut into pieces
- 2 garlic cloves, minced
- 15ml olive oil
- 239g frozen mix vegetables
- 1 tbsp Italian seasoning
- ½ tsp chilli powder
- ½ tsp garlic powder
- Pepper
- Salt

Directions:
1. In a bowl, toss chicken with remaining ingredients until well coated.
2. Insert a crisper plate in the Instant air fryer baskets.
3. Add chicken and vegetables in both baskets.
4. Select zone 1 then select "air fry" mode and set the temperature to 390 degrees F for 10 minutes. Press "match" to match zone 2 settings to zone 1. Press "start/stop" to begin.

Nutrition:
- (Per serving) Calories 221 | Fat 7.6g | Sodium 126mg | Carbs 10.6g | Fiber 3.3g | Sugar 2.7g | Protein 26.3g

Teriyaki Chicken Skewers

Servings: 4
Cooking Time: 16 Minutes
Ingredients:
- 455g boneless chicken thighs, cubed
- 237ml teriyaki marinade
- 16 small wooden skewers
- Sesame seeds for rolling
- Teriyaki Marinade
- ⅓ cup soy sauce
- 59ml chicken broth
- ½ orange, juiced
- 2 tablespoons brown sugar
- 1 teaspoon ginger, grated
- 1 clove garlic, grated

Directions:
1. Blend teriyaki marinade ingredients in a blender.
2. Add chicken and its marinade to a Ziplock bag.
3. Seal this bag, shake it well and refrigerate for 30 minutes.
4. Thread the chicken on the wooden skewers.
5. Place these skewers in the air fryer baskets.
6. Return the air fryer basket 1 to Zone 1, and basket 2 to Zone 2 of the Instant 2-Basket Air Fryer.
7. Choose the "Air Fry" mode for Zone 1 at 350 degrees F and 16 minutes of cooking time.
8. Select the "MATCH COOK" option to copy the settings for Zone 2.
9. Initiate cooking by pressing the START/PAUSE BUTTON.
10. Flip the skewers once cooked halfway through.
11. Garnish with sesame seeds.
12. Serve warm.

Nutrition:
- (Per serving) Calories 456 | Fat 16.4g | Sodium 1321mg | Carbs 19.2g | Fiber 2.2g | Sugar 4.2g | Protein 55.2g

Bbq Cheddar-stuffed Chicken Breasts

Servings: 2
Cooking Time: 25 Minutes
Ingredients:
- 3 strips cooked bacon, divided
- 2 ounces cheddar cheese, cubed, divided
- ¼ cup BBQ sauce, divided
- 2 (4-ounces) skinless, boneless chicken breasts
- Salt and ground black pepper, to taste

Directions:
1. In a mixing bowl, combine the cooked bacon, cheddar cheese, and 1 tablespoon BBQ sauce.
2. Make a horizontal 1-inch cut at the top of each chicken breast with a long, sharp knife, producing a little interior pouch. Fill each breast with an equal amount of the bacon-cheese mixture. Wrap the remaining bacon strips around each chicken breast. Coat the chicken breasts with the leftover BBQ sauce and lay them in a baking dish.
3. Install a crisper plate in both drawers. Place half the chicken breasts in zone 1 and half in zone 2, then insert the drawers into the unit.
4. Select zone 1, select AIR FRY, set temperature to 390 degrees F/ 200 degrees C, and set time to 22 minutes. Select MATCH to match zone 2 settings to zone 1. Press the START/STOP button to begin cooking.
5. When the time reaches 11 minutes, press START/STOP to pause the unit. Remove the drawers and flip the chicken. Re-insert drawers into the unit and press START/STOP to resume cooking.
6. When cooking is complete, remove the chicken breasts.

Nutrition:
- (Per serving) Calories 379 | Fat 12.8g | Sodium 906mg | Carbs 11.1g | Fiber 0.4g | Sugar 8.3g | Protein 37.7g

Juicy Duck Breast

Servings: 1
Cooking Time: 20 Minutes
Ingredients:
- ½ duck breast
- Salt and black pepper, to taste
- 2 tablespoons plum sauce

Directions:
1. Rub the duck breast with black pepper and salt.
2. Place the duck breast in air fryer basket 1 and add plum sauce on top.
3. Return the basket to the Instant 2 Baskets Air Fryer.
4. Choose the "Air Fry" mode for Zone 1 and set the temperature to 400 degrees F and 20 minutes of cooking time.
5. Initiate cooking by pressing the START/PAUSE BUTTON.
6. Flip the duck breast once cooked halfway through.
7. Serve warm.

Nutrition:
- (Per serving) Calories 379 | Fat 19g | Sodium 184mg | Carbs 12.3g | Fiber 0.6g | Sugar 2g | Protein 37.7g

Chicken With Pineapple And Peach

Servings: 4
Cooking Time: 14 To 15 Minutes
Ingredients:
- 1 (450 g) low-sodium boneless, skinless chicken breasts, cut into 1-inch pieces
- 1 medium red onion, chopped
- 1 (230 g) can pineapple chunks, drained, 60 ml juice reserved
- 1 tablespoon peanut oil or safflower oil
- 1 peach, peeled, pitted, and cubed
- 1 tablespoon cornflour
- ½ teaspoon ground ginger
- ¼ teaspoon ground allspice
- Brown rice, cooked (optional)

Directions:
1. Preheat the air fryer to 195°C.
2. In a medium metal bowl, mix the chicken, red onion, pineapple, and peanut oil. Bake in the air fryer for 9 minutes. Remove and stir.
3. Add the peach and return the bowl to the air fryer. Bake for 3 minutes more. Remove and stir again.
4. In a small bowl, whisk the reserved pineapple juice, the cornflour, ginger, and allspice well. Add to the chicken mixture and stir to combine.
5. Bake for 2 to 3 minutes more, or until the chicken reaches an internal temperature of 75°C on a meat thermometer and the sauce is slightly thickened.
6. Serve immediately over hot cooked brown rice, if desired.

Crusted Chicken Breast

Servings: 4
Cooking Time: 28 Minutes
Ingredients:
- 2 large eggs, beaten
- ½ cup all-purpose flour
- 1 ¼ cups panko bread crumbs
- ⅔ cup Parmesan, grated
- 4 teaspoons lemon zest
- 2 teaspoons dried oregano
- Salt, to taste
- 1 teaspoon cayenne pepper
- Freshly black pepper, to taste
- 4 boneless skinless chicken breasts

Directions:
1. Beat eggs in one shallow bowl and spread flour in another shallow bowl.
2. Mix panko with oregano, lemon zest, Parmesan, cayenne, oregano, salt, and black pepper in another shallow bowl.
3. First, coat the chicken with flour first, then dip it in the eggs and coat them with panko mixture.
4. Arrange the prepared chicken in the two crisper plates.
5. Return the crisper plate to the Instant Dual Zone Air Fryer.
6. Choose the Air Fry mode for Zone 1 and set the temperature to 390 degrees F and the time to 28 minutes|
7. Select the "MATCH" button to copy the settings for Zone 2.
8. Initiate cooking by pressing the START/STOP button.
9. Flip the half-cooked chicken and continue cooking for 5 minutes until golden.
10. Serve warm.

Jerk Chicken Thighs

Servings: 6
Cooking Time: 15 To 20 Minutes
Ingredients:
- 2 teaspoons ground coriander
- 1 teaspoon ground allspice
- 1 teaspoon cayenne pepper
- 1 teaspoon ground ginger
- 1 teaspoon salt
- 1 teaspoon dried thyme
- ½ teaspoon ground cinnamon
- ½ teaspoon ground nutmeg
- 900 g boneless chicken thighs, skin on
- 2 tablespoons olive oil

Directions:
1. In a small bowl, combine the coriander, allspice, cayenne, ginger, salt, thyme, cinnamon, and nutmeg. Stir until thoroughly combined.
2. Place the chicken in a baking dish and use paper towels to pat dry. Thoroughly coat both sides of the chicken with the spice mixture. Cover and refrigerate for at least 2 hours, preferably overnight.
3. Preheat the air fryer to 180°C.
4. Arrange the chicken in a single layer in the two air fryer drawers and lightly coat with the olive oil. Pausing halfway through the cooking time to flip the chicken, air fry for 15 to 20 minutes, until a thermometer inserted into the thickest part registers 76°C.

Chicken Leg Piece

Servings: 1
Cooking Time: 25

Ingredients:
- 1 teaspoon of onion powder
- 1 teaspoon of paprika powder
- 1 teaspoon of garlic powder
- Salt and black pepper, to taste
- 1 tablespoon of Italian seasoning
- 1 teaspoon of celery seeds
- 2 eggs, whisked
- 1/3 cup buttermilk
- 1 cup of corn flour
- 1 pound of chicken leg

Directions:
1. Take a bowl and whisk egg along with pepper, salt, and buttermilk.
2. Set it aside for further use.
3. Mix all the spices in a small separate bowl.
4. Dredge the chicken in egg wash then dredge it in seasoning.
5. Coat the chicken legs with oil spray.
6. At the end dust it with the corn flour.
7. Divide the leg pieces into two zones.
8. Set zone 1 basket to 400 degrees F, for 25 minutes.
9. Select MATCH for zone 2 basket.
10. Let the air fryer do the magic.
11. Once it's done, serve and enjoy.

Nutrition:
- (Per serving) Calories 1511| Fat 52.3g| Sodium615 mg | Carbs 100g | Fiber 9.2g | Sugar 8.1g | Protein 154.2g

Ranch Turkey Tenders With Roasted Vegetable Salad

Servings: 4
Cooking Time: 20 Minutes

Ingredients:
- FOR THE TURKEY TENDERS
- 1 pound turkey tenderloin
- ¼ cup ranch dressing
- ½ cup panko bread crumbs
- Nonstick cooking spray
- FOR THE VEGETABLE SALAD
- 1 large sweet potato, peeled and diced
- 1 zucchini, diced
- 1 red bell pepper, diced
- 1 small red onion, sliced
- 1 tablespoon vegetable oil
- ¼ teaspoon kosher salt
- ½ teaspoon freshly ground black pepper
- 2 cups baby spinach
- ½ cup store-bought balsamic vinaigrette
- ¼ cup chopped walnuts

Directions:
1. To prep the turkey tenders: Slice the turkey crosswise into 16 strips. Brush both sides of each strip with ranch dressing, then coat with the panko. Press the bread crumbs into the turkey to help them adhere. Mist both sides of the strips with cooking spray.
2. To prep the vegetables: In a large bowl, combine the sweet potato, zucchini, bell pepper, onion, and vegetable oil. Stir well to coat the vegetables. Season with the salt and black pepper.
3. To cook the turkey and vegetables:
4. Install a crisper plate in the Zone 1 basket. Place the turkey tenders in the basket in a single layer and insert the basket in the unit. Place the vegetables in the Zone 2 basket and insert the basket in the unit.
5. Select Zone 1, select AIR FRY, set the temperature to 375°F, and set the time to 20 minutes.
6. Select Zone 2, select ROAST, set the temperature to 400°F, and set the time to 20 minutes. Select SMART FINISH.
7. Press START/PAUSE to begin cooking.
8. When both timers read 10 minutes, press START/PAUSE. Remove the Zone 1 basket and use silicone-tipped tongs to flip the turkey tenders. Reinsert the basket in the unit. Remove the Zone 2 basket and shake to redistribute the vegetables. Reinsert the basket and press START/PAUSE to resume cooking.
9. When cooking is complete, the turkey will be golden brown and cooked through and the vegetables will be fork-tender.
10. Place the spinach in a large serving bowl. Mix in the roasted vegetables and balsamic vinaigrette. Sprinkle with walnuts. Serve warm with the turkey tenders.

Chicken And Vegetable Fajitas

Servings: 6
Cooking Time: 23 Minutes
Ingredients:
- Chicken:
- 450 g boneless, skinless chicken thighs, cut crosswise into thirds
- 1 tablespoon vegetable oil
- 4½ teaspoons taco seasoning
- Vegetables:
- 50 g sliced onion
- 150 g sliced bell pepper
- 1 or 2 jalapeños, quartered lengthwise
- 1 tablespoon vegetable oil
- ½ teaspoon kosher salt
- ½ teaspoon ground cumin
- For Serving:
- Tortillas
- Sour cream
- Shredded cheese
- Guacamole
- Salsa

Directions:
1. For the chicken: In a medium bowl, toss together the chicken, vegetable oil, and taco seasoning to coat. 2. For the vegetables: In a separate bowl, toss together the onion, bell pepper, jalapeño, vegetable oil, salt, and cumin to coat. 3. Place the chicken in the air fryer basket. Set the air fryer to (190°C for 10 minutes. Add the vegetables to the basket, toss everything together to blend the seasonings, and set the air fryer for 13 minutes more. Use a meat thermometer to ensure the chicken has reached an internal temperature of 75°C. 4. Transfer the chicken and vegetables to a serving platter. Serve with tortillas and the desired fajita fixings.

Goat Cheese–stuffed Chicken Breast With Broiled Zucchini And Cherry Tomatoes

Servings: 4
Cooking Time: 25 Minutes
Ingredients:
- FOR THE STUFFED CHICKEN BREASTS
- 2 ounces soft goat cheese
- 1 tablespoon minced fresh parsley
- ½ teaspoon minced garlic
- 4 boneless, skinless chicken breasts (6 ounces each)
- 1 tablespoon vegetable oil
- ½ teaspoon Italian seasoning
- ½ teaspoon kosher salt
- ½ teaspoon freshly ground black pepper
- FOR THE ZUCCHINI AND TOMATOES
- 1 pound zucchini, diced
- 1 cup cherry tomatoes, halved
- 1 tablespoon vegetable oil
- ½ teaspoon kosher salt
- ¼ teaspoon freshly ground black pepper

Directions:
1. To prep the stuffed chicken breasts:
2. In a small bowl, combine the goat cheese, parsley, and garlic. Mix well.
3. Cut a deep slit into the fatter side of each chicken breast to create a pocket . Stuff each breast with the goat cheese mixture. Use a toothpick to secure the opening of the chicken, if needed.
4. Brush the outside of the chicken breasts with the oil and season with the Italian seasoning, salt, and black pepper.
5. To prep the zucchini and tomatoes: In a large bowl, combine the zucchini, tomatoes, and oil. Mix to coat. Season with salt and black pepper.
6. To cook the chicken and vegetables:
7. Install a crisper plate in each of the two baskets. Insert a broil rack in the Zone 2 basket over the crisper plate. Place the chicken in the Zone 1 basket and insert the basket in the unit. Place the vegetables on the broiler rack in the Zone 2 basket and insert the basket in the unit.
8. Select Zone 1, select AIR FRY, set the temperature to 390°F, and set the time to 25 minutes.
9. Select Zone 2, select AIR BROIL, set the temperature to 450°F, and set the time to 10 minutes. Select SMART FINISH.
10. Press START/PAUSE to begin cooking.
11. When cooking is complete, the chicken will be golden brown and cooked through and the zucchini will be soft and slightly charred. Serve hot.

Crispy Fried Quail

Servings: 8
Cooking Time: 6 Minutes
Ingredients:
- 8 boneless quail breasts
- 2 tablespoons Sichuan pepper dry rub mix
- ¾ cup rice flour
- ¼ cup all-purpose flour
- 2-3 cups peanut oil
- Garnish
- Sliced jalapenos
- Fresh lime wedges
- Fresh coriander

Directions:
1. Split the quail breasts in half.
2. Mix Sichuan mix with flours in a bowl.
3. Coat the quail breasts with flour mixture and place in the air fryer baskets.
4. Return the air fryer basket 1 to Zone 1, and basket 2 to Zone 2 of the Instant 2-Basket Air Fryer.
5. Choose the "Air Fry" mode for Zone 1 at 300 degrees F and 6 minutes of cooking time.
6. Select the "MATCH COOK" option to copy the settings for Zone 2.
7. Initiate cooking by pressing the START/PAUSE BUTTON.
8. Flip the quail breasts once cooked halfway through.
9. Serve warm.

Nutrition:
- (Per serving) Calories 351 | Fat 11g |Sodium 150mg | Carbs 3.3g | Fiber 0.2g | Sugar 1g | Protein 33.2g

Yummy Chicken Breasts

Servings:2
Cooking Time:25
Ingredients:
- 4 large chicken breasts, 6 ounces each
- 2 tablespoons of oil bay seasoning
- 1 tablespoon Montreal chicken seasoning
- 1 teaspoon of thyme
- 1/2 teaspoon of paprika
- Salt, to taste
- oil spray, for greasing

Directions:
1. Season the chicken breast pieces with the listed seasoning and let them rest for 40 minutes.
2. Grease both sides of the chicken breast pieces with oil spray.
3. Divide the chicken breast piece between both baskets.
4. Set zone 1 to AIRFRY mode at 400 degrees F, for 15 minutes.
5. Select the MATCH button for another basket.
6. Select pause and take out the baskets and flip the chicken breast pieces, after 15 minutes.
7. Select the zones to 400 degrees F for 10 more minutes using the MATCH cook button.
8. Once it's done serve.

Nutrition:
- (Per serving) Calories 711| Fat 27.7g| Sodium 895mg | Carbs 1.6g | Fiber 0.4g | Sugar 0.1g | Protein 106.3g

Honey-glazed Chicken Thighs

Servings: 4
Cooking Time: 14 Minutes
Ingredients:
- Oil, for spraying
- 4 boneless, skinless chicken thighs, fat trimmed
- 3 tablespoons soy sauce
- 1 tablespoon balsamic vinegar
- 2 teaspoons honey
- 2 teaspoons minced garlic
- 1 teaspoon ground ginger

Directions:
1. Preheat the zone 1 air fryer drawer to 200ºC. Line the zone 1 air fryer drawer with parchment and spray lightly with oil.
2. Place the chicken in the prepared drawer.
3. Cook for 7 minutes, flip, and cook for another 7 minutes, or until the internal temperature reaches 76ºC and the juices run clear.
4. In a small saucepan, combine the soy sauce, balsamic vinegar, honey, garlic, and ginger and cook over low heat for 1 to 2 minutes, until warmed through.
5. Transfer the chicken to a serving plate and drizzle with the sauce just before serving.

Air Fried Chicken Potatoes With Sun-dried Tomato

Servings: 2
Cooking Time: 25 Minutes
Ingredients:
- 2 teaspoons minced fresh oregano, divided
- 2 teaspoons minced fresh thyme, divided
- 2 teaspoons extra-virgin olive oil, plus extra as needed
- 450 g fingerling potatoes, unpeeled
- 2 (340 g) bone-in split chicken breasts, trimmed
- 1 garlic clove, minced
- 15 g oil-packed sun-dried tomatoes, patted dry and chopped
- 1½ tablespoons red wine vinegar
- 1 tablespoon capers, rinsed and minced
- 1 small shallot, minced
- Salt and ground black pepper, to taste

Directions:
1. Preheat the zone 1 air fryer drawer to 180°C.
2. Combine 1 teaspoon of oregano, 1 teaspoon of thyme, ¼ teaspoon of salt, ¼ teaspoon of ground black pepper, 1 teaspoons of olive oil in a large bowl. Add the potatoes and toss to coat well.
3. Combine the chicken with remaining thyme, oregano, and olive oil. Sprinkle with garlic, salt, and pepper. Toss to coat well.
4. Place the potatoes in the preheated air fryer drawer, then arrange the chicken on top of the potatoes.
5. Air fry for 25 minutes or until the internal temperature of the chicken reaches at least 76°C and the potatoes are wilted. Flip the chicken and potatoes halfway through.
6. Meanwhile, combine the sun-dried tomatoes, vinegar, capers, and shallot in a separate large bowl. Sprinkle with salt and ground black pepper. Toss to mix well.
7. Remove the chicken and potatoes from the air fryer and allow to cool for 10 minutes. Serve with the sun-dried tomato mix.

Chicken And Broccoli

Servings: 4
Cooking Time: 15 Minutes
Ingredients:
- 1-pound boneless, skinless chicken breast or thighs, cut into 1-inch bite-sized pieces
- ¼ –½ pound broccoli, cut into florets (1–2 cups)
- ½ medium onion, cut into thick slices
- 3 tablespoons olive oil or grape seed oil
- ½ teaspoon garlic powder
- 1 tablespoon fresh minced ginger
- 1 tablespoon low-sodium soy sauce
- 1 tablespoon rice vinegar
- 1 teaspoon sesame oil
- 2 teaspoons hot sauce (optional)
- ½ teaspoon sea salt, or to taste
- Black pepper, to taste
- Lemon wedges, for serving (optional)

Directions:
1. Combine the oil, garlic powder, ginger, soy sauce, rice vinegar, sesame oil, optional spicy sauce, salt, and pepper in a large mixing bowl.
2. Put the chicken in a separate bowl.
3. In a separate bowl, combine the broccoli and onions.
4. Divide the marinade between the two bowls and toss to evenly coat each.
5. Install a crisper plate into both drawers. Place the broccoli in the zone 1 drawer, then insert the drawer into the unit. Place the chicken breasts in the zone 2 drawer, then insert the drawer into the unit.
6. Select zone 1, select AIR FRY, set temperature to 390 degrees F/ 200 degrees C, and set time to 10 minutes. Select zone 2, select AIR FRY, set temperature to 390 degrees F/ 200 degrees C, and set time to 20 minutes. Select SYNC. Press the START/STOP button to begin cooking.
7. When zone 2 time reaches 9 minutes, press START/STOP to pause the unit. Remove the drawer and toss the chicken. Re-insert the drawer into the unit and press START/STOP to resume cooking.
8. When cooking is complete, serve the chicken breasts and broccoli while still hot.
9. Add additional salt and pepper to taste. Squeeze optional fresh lemon juice on top and serve warm.

Nutrition:
- (Per serving) Calories 224 | Fat 15.8g | Sodium 203mg | Carbs 4g | Fiber 1g | Sugar 1g | Protein 25g

Bacon-wrapped Chicken

Servings: 2
Cooking Time: 28 Minutes
Ingredients:
- Butter:
- ½ stick butter softened
- ½ garlic clove, minced
- ¼ teaspoon dried thyme
- ¼ teaspoon dried basil
- ⅛ teaspoon coarse salt
- 1 pinch black pepper, ground
- ⅓ lb. thick-cut bacon
- 1 ½ lbs. boneless skinless chicken thighs
- 2 teaspoons garlic, minced

Directions:
1. Mix garlic softened butter with thyme, salt, basil, and black pepper in a bowl.
2. Add butter mixture on a piece of wax paper and roll it up tightly to make a butter log.
3. Place the log in the refrigerator for 2 hours.
4. Spray one bacon strip on a piece of wax paper.
5. Place each chicken thigh on top of one bacon strip and rub it with garlic.
6. Make a slit in the chicken thigh and add a teaspoon of butter to the chicken.
7. Wrap the bacon around the chicken thigh.
8. Repeat those same steps with all the chicken thighs.
9. Place the bacon-wrapped chicken thighs in the two crisper plates.
10. Return the crisper plates to the Instant Dual Zone Air Fryer.
11. Choose the Air Fry mode for Zone 1 and set the temperature to 390 degrees F and the time to 28 minutes|
12. Select the "MATCH" button to copy the settings for Zone 2.
13. Initiate cooking by pressing the START/STOP button.
14. Flip the chicken once cooked halfway through, and resume cooking.
15. Serve warm.

Roasted Garlic Chicken Pizza With Cauliflower "wings"

Servings: 4
Cooking Time: 25 Minutes
Ingredients:
- FOR THE PIZZA
- 2 prebaked rectangular pizza crusts or flatbreads
- 2 tablespoons olive oil
- 1 tablespoon minced garlic
- 1½ cups shredded part-skim mozzarella cheese
- 6 ounces boneless, skinless chicken breast, thinly sliced
- ¼ teaspoon red pepper flakes (optional)
- FOR THE CAULIFLOWER "WINGS"
- 4 cups cauliflower florets
- 1 tablespoon vegetable oil
- ½ cup Buffalo wing sauce

Directions:
1. To prep the pizza:
2. Trim the pizza crusts to fit in the air fryer basket, if necessary.
3. Brush the top of each crust with the oil and sprinkle with the garlic. Top the crusts with the mozzarella, chicken, and red pepper flakes .
4. To prep the cauliflower "wings": In a large bowl, combine the cauliflower and oil and toss to coat the florets.
5. To cook the pizza and "wings":
6. Install a crisper plate in each of the two baskets. Place one pizza in the Zone 1 basket and insert the basket in the unit. Place the cauliflower in the Zone 2 basket and insert the basket in the unit.
7. Select Zone 1, select ROAST, set the temperature to 375°F, and set the time to 25 minutes.
8. Select Zone 2, select AIR FRY, set the temperature to 390°F, and set the time to 25 minutes. Select SMART FINISH.
9. Press START/PAUSE to begin cooking.
10. When the Zone 1 timer reads 13 minutes, press START/PAUSE. Remove the basket. Transfer the pizza to a cutting board . Add the second pizza to the basket. Reinsert the basket in the unit and press START/PAUSE to resume cooking.
11. When the Zone 2 timer reads 5 minutes, press START/PAUSE. Remove the basket and add the Buffalo wing sauce to the cauliflower. Shake well to evenly coat the cauliflower in the sauce. Reinsert the basket and press START/PAUSE to resume cooking.
12. When cooking is complete, the cauliflower will be crisp on the outside and tender inside, and the chicken on the second pizza will be cooked through and the cheese melted.
13. Cut each pizza into 4 slices. Serve with the cauliflower "wings" on the side.

Glazed Thighs With French Fries

Servings: 3
Cooking Time: 35
Ingredients:
- 2 tablespoons of Soy Sauce
- Salt, to taste
- 1 teaspoon of Worcestershire Sauce
- 2 teaspoons Brown Sugar
- 1 teaspoon of Ginger, paste
- 1 teaspoon of Garlic, paste
- 6 Boneless Chicken Thighs
- 1 pound of hand-cut potato fries
- 2 tablespoons of canola oil

Directions:
1. Coat the French fries well with canola oil.
2. Season it with salt.
3. In a small bowl, combine the soy sauce, Worcestershire sauce, brown sugar, ginger, and garlic.
4. Place the chicken in this marinade and let it sit for 40 minutes.
5. Put the chicken thighs into the zone 1 basket and fries into the zone 2 basket.
6. Press button 1 for the first basket, and set it to ROAST mode at 350 degrees F for 35 minutes.
7. For the second basket hit 2 and set time to 30 minutes at 360 degrees F, by selecting AIR FRY mode.
8. Once the cooking cycle completely take out the fries and chicken and serve it hot.

Nutrition:
- (Per serving) Calories 858| Fat39g | Sodium 1509mg | Carbs 45.6g | Fiber 4.4g | Sugar3 g | Protein 90g

Bell Pepper Stuffed Chicken Roll-ups

Servings: 4
Cooking Time: 12 Minutes
Ingredients:
- 2 (115 g) boneless, skinless chicken breasts, slice in half horizontally
- 1 tablespoon olive oil
- Juice of ½ lime
- 2 tablespoons taco seasoning
- ½ green bell pepper, cut into strips
- ½ red bell pepper, cut into strips
- ¼ onion, sliced

Directions:
1. Preheat the air fryer to 200°C.
2. Unfold the chicken breast slices on a clean work surface. Rub with olive oil, then drizzle with lime juice and sprinkle with taco seasoning.
3. Top the chicken slices with equal amount of bell peppers and onion. Roll them up and secure with toothpicks.
4. Arrange the chicken roll-ups in the preheated air fryer. Air fry for 12 minutes or until the internal temperature of the chicken reaches at least 75°C. Flip the chicken roll-ups halfway through.
5. Remove the chicken from the air fryer. Discard the toothpicks and serve immediately.

Balsamic Duck Breast

Servings: 2
Cooking Time: 20 Minutes
Ingredients:
- 2 duck breasts
- 1 teaspoon parsley
- Salt and black pepper, to taste
- Marinade:
- 1 tablespoon olive oil
- ½ teaspoon French mustard
- 1 teaspoon dried garlic
- 2 teaspoons honey
- ½ teaspoon balsamic vinegar

Directions:
1. Mix olive oil, mustard, garlic, honey, and balsamic vinegar in a bowl.
2. Add duck breasts to the marinade and rub well.
3. Place one duck breast in each crisper plate.
4. Return the crisper plates to the Instant Dual Zone Air Fryer.
5. Choose the Air Fry mode for Zone 1 and set the temperature to 360 degrees F and the time to 20 minutes|
6. Select the "MATCH" button to copy the settings for Zone 2.
7. Initiate cooking by pressing the START/STOP button.
8. Flip the duck breasts once cooked halfway through, then resume cooking.
9. Serve warm.

Cornish Hen With Asparagus

Servings: 2
Cooking Time: 45

Ingredients:
- 10 spears of asparagus
- Salt and black pepper, to taste
- 1 Cornish hen
- Salt, to taste
- Black pepper, to taste
- 1 teaspoon of Paprika
- Coconut spray, for greasing
- 2 lemons, sliced

Directions:
1. Wash and pat dry the asparagus and coat it with coconut oil spray.
2. Sprinkle salt on the asparagus and place inside the first basket of the air fryer.
3. Next, take the Cornish hen and rub it well with the salt, black pepper, and paprika.
4. Oil sprays the Cornish hen and place in the second air fryer basket.
5. Press button 1 for the first basket and set it to AIR FRY mode at 350 degrees F, for 8 minutes.
6. For the second basket hit 2 and set the time to 45 minutes at 350 degrees F, by selecting the ROAST mode.
7. To start cooking, hit the smart finish button and press hit start.
8. Once the 6 minutes pass press 1 and pause and take out the asparagus.
9. Once the chicken cooking cycle complete, press 2 and hit pause.
10. Take out the Basket of chicken and let it transfer to the serving plate
11. Serve the chicken with roasted asparagus and slices of lemon.
12. Serve hot and enjoy.

Nutrition:
- (Per serving) Calories 192| Fat 4.7g| Sodium 151mg | Carbs10.7 g | Fiber 4.6g | Sugar 3.8g | Protein 30g

Chicken Caprese

Servings: 4
Cooking Time: 10 Minutes

Ingredients:
- 4 chicken breast cutlets
- 1 teaspoon Italian seasoning
- 1 teaspoon salt
- ½ teaspoon black pepper
- 4 slices fresh mozzarella cheese
- 1 large tomato, sliced
- Basil and balsamic vinegar to garnish

Directions:
1. Pat dry the chicken cutlets with a kitchen towel.
2. Rub the chicken with Italian seasoning, black pepper and salt.
3. Place two chicken breasts in each air fryer basket.
4. Return the air fryer basket 1 to Zone 1, and basket 2 to Zone 2 of the Instant 2-Basket Air Fryer.
5. Choose the "Air Fry" mode for Zone 1 at 375 degrees F and 10 minutes of cooking time.
6. Select the "MATCH COOK" option to copy the settings for Zone 2.
7. Initiate cooking by pressing the START/PAUSE BUTTON.
8. After 10 minutes top each chicken breast with a slice of cheese and tomato slices.
9. Return the baskets to the Instant 2 Baskets Air Fryer and air fry for 5 another minutes.
10. Garnish with balsamic vinegar and basil.
11. Serve warm.

Nutrition:
- (Per serving) Calories 502 | Fat 25g |Sodium 230mg | Carbs 1.5g | Fiber 0.2g | Sugar 0.4g | Protein 64.1g

Chicken Legs With Leeks

Servings: 6
Cooking Time: 18 Minutes

Ingredients:
- 2 leeks, sliced
- 2 large-sized tomatoes, chopped
- 3 cloves garlic, minced
- ½ teaspoon dried oregano
- 6 chicken legs, boneless and skinless
- ½ teaspoon smoked cayenne pepper
- 2 tablespoons olive oil
- A freshly ground nutmeg

Directions:
1. In a mixing dish, thoroughly combine all ingredients, minus the leeks. Place in the refrigerator and let it marinate overnight.
2. Lay the leeks onto the bottom of the two air fryer drawers. Top with the chicken legs.
3. Roast chicken legs at 190°C for 18 minutes, turning halfway through. Serve with hoisin sauce.

Wild Rice And Kale Stuffed Chicken Thighs

Servings: 4
Cooking Time: 22 Minutes
Ingredients:
- 4 boneless, skinless chicken thighs
- 250 g cooked wild rice
- 35 g chopped kale
- 2 garlic cloves, minced
- 1 teaspoon salt
- Juice of 1 lemon
- 100 g crumbled feta
- Olive oil cooking spray
- 1 tablespoon olive oi

Directions:
1. Preheat the air fryer to 192°C.
2. Place the chicken thighs between two pieces of plastic wrap, and using a meat mallet or a rolling pin, pound them out to about ¼-inch thick.
3. In a medium bowl, combine the rice, kale, garlic, salt, and lemon juice and mix well.
4. Place a quarter of the rice mixture into the middle of each chicken thigh, then sprinkle 2 tablespoons of feta over the filling.
5. Spray the two air fryer drawers with olive oil cooking spray.
6. Fold the sides of the chicken thigh over the filling, and then gently place each of them seam-side down into the two air fryer drawers. Brush each stuffed chicken thigh with olive oil.
7. Roast the stuffed chicken thighs for 12 minutes, then turn them over and cook for an additional 10 minutes, or until the internal temperature reaches 76°C.

Chipotle Drumsticks

Servings: 4
Cooking Time: 20 Minutes
Ingredients:
- 1 tablespoon tomato paste
- ½ teaspoon chipotle powder
- ¼ teaspoon apple cider vinegar
- ¼ teaspoon garlic powder
- 8 chicken drumsticks
- ½ teaspoon salt
- ⅛ teaspoon ground black pepper

Directions:
1. In a small bowl, combine tomato paste, chipotle powder, vinegar, and garlic powder.
2. Sprinkle drumsticks with salt and pepper, then place into a large bowl and pour in tomato paste mixture. Toss or stir to evenly coat all drumsticks in mixture.
3. Place drumsticks into two ungreased air fryer baskets. Adjust the temperature to 200°C and air fry for 25 minutes, turning drumsticks halfway through cooking. Drumsticks will be dark red with an internal temperature of at least 75°C when done. Serve warm.

Chicken And Potatoes

Servings: 2
Cooking Time: 10 Minutes
Ingredients:
- 2 potatoes, diced
- 2 chicken breasts, diced
- 4 cloves garlic crushed
- 2 teaspoons smoked paprika
- ½ teaspoon red chili flakes
- 1 teaspoon fresh thyme
- 1 teaspoon salt
- ¼ teaspoon black pepper
- 2 tablespoons olive oil

Directions:
1. Rub chicken with half of the salt, black pepper, oil, thyme, red chili flakes, paprika and garlic.
2. Mix potatoes with remaining spices, oil and garlic in a bowl.
3. Add chicken to one air fryer basket and potatoes the second basket.
4. Return the air fryer basket 1 to Zone 1, and basket 2 to Zone 2 of the Instant 2-Basket Air Fryer.
5. Choose the "Air Fry" mode for Zone 1 at 375 degrees F and 10 minutes of cooking time.
6. Select the "MATCH COOK" option to copy the settings for Zone 2.
7. Initiate cooking by pressing the START/PAUSE BUTTON.
8. Flip the chicken and toss potatoes once cooked halfway through.
9. Garnish with chopped parsley.
10. Serve chicken with the potatoes.

Nutrition:
- (Per serving) Calories 374 | Fat 13g | Sodium 552mg | Carbs 25g | Fiber 1.2g | Sugar 1.2g | Protein 37.7g

Thai Chicken With Cucumber And Chili Salad

Servings: 6
Cooking Time: 25 Minutes
Ingredients:
- 2 (570 g) small chickens, giblets discarded
- 1 tablespoon fish sauce
- 6 tablespoons chopped fresh coriander
- 2 teaspoons lime zest
- 1 teaspoon ground coriander
- 2 garlic cloves, minced
- 2 tablespoons packed light brown sugar
- 2 teaspoons vegetable oil
- Salt and ground black pepper, to taste
- 1 English cucumber, halved lengthwise and sliced thin
- 1 Thai chili, stemmed, deseeded, and minced
- 2 tablespoons chopped dry-roasted peanuts
- 1 small shallot, sliced thinly
- 1 tablespoon lime juice
- Lime wedges, for serving
- Cooking spray

Directions:
1. Arrange a chicken on a clean work surface, remove the backbone with kitchen shears, then pound the chicken breast to flat. Cut the breast in half. Repeat with the remaining chicken.
2. Loose the breast and thigh skin with your fingers, then pat the chickens dry and pierce about 10 holes into the fat deposits of the chickens. Tuck the wings under the chickens.
3. Combine 2 teaspoons of fish sauce, coriander, lime zest, coriander, garlic, 4 teaspoons of sugar, 1 teaspoon of vegetable oil, ½ teaspoon of salt, and ⅛ teaspoon of ground black pepper in a small bowl. Stir to mix well.
4. Rub the fish sauce mixture under the breast and thigh skin of the game chickens, then let sit for 10 minutes to marinate.
5. Preheat the air fryer to 200°C. Spritz the two air fryer baskets with cooking spray.
6. Arrange the marinated chickens in the preheated air fryer, skin side down.
7. Air fry for 15 minutes, then gently turn the game hens over and air fry for 10 more minutes or until the skin is golden brown and the internal temperature of the chickens reads at least 75°C.
8. Meanwhile, combine all the remaining ingredients, except for the lime wedges, in a large bowl and sprinkle with salt and black pepper. Toss to mix well.
9. Transfer the fried chickens on a large plate, then sit the salad aside and squeeze the lime wedges over before serving.

Spicy Chicken

Servings: 40
Cooking Time: 35
Ingredients:
- 4 chicken thighs
- 2 cups of butter milk
- 4 chicken legs
- 2 cups of flour
- Salt and black pepper, to taste
- 2 tablespoons garlic powder
- ½ teaspoon onion powder
- 1 teaspoon poultry seasoning
- 1 teaspoon cumin
- 2 tablespoons paprika
- 1 tablespoon olive oil

Directions:
1. Take a bowl and add buttermilk to it.
2. Soak the chicken thighs and chicken legs in the buttermilk for 2 hours.
3. Mix flour, all the seasonings, and olive oil in a small bowl.
4. Take out the chicken pieces from the buttermilk mixture and then dredge them into the flour mixture.
5. Repeat the steps for all the pieces and then arrange them into both the air fryer basket.
6. Set the timer for both the basket by selecting a roast mode for 35-40 minutes at 350 degrees F.
7. Once the cooking cycle complete select the pause button and then take out the basket.
8. Serve and enjoy.

Nutrition:
- (Per serving) Calories 624| Fat17.6 g| Sodium300 mg | Carbs 60g | Fiber 3.5g | Sugar 7.7g | Protein54.2 g

Spicy Chicken Sandwiches With "fried" Pickles

Servings: 4
Cooking Time: 18 Minutes
Ingredients:
- FOR THE CHICKEN SANDWICHES
- 2 tablespoons all-purpose flour
- 2 large eggs
- 2 teaspoons Louisiana-style hot sauce
- 1 cup panko bread crumbs
- 1 teaspoon paprika
- ½ teaspoon garlic powder
- ¼ teaspoon salt
- ¼ teaspoon freshly ground black pepper
- ¼ teaspoon cayenne pepper (optional)
- 4 thin-sliced chicken cutlets (4 ounces each)
- 2 teaspoons vegetable oil
- 4 hamburger rolls
- FOR THE PICKLES
- 1 cup dill pickle chips, drained
- 1 large egg
- ½ cup panko bread crumbs
- Nonstick cooking spray
- ½ cup ranch dressing, for serving (optional)

Directions:
1. To prep the sandwiches:
2. Set up a breading station with three small shallow bowls. Place the flour in the first bowl. In the second bowl, whisk together the eggs and hot sauce. Combine the panko, paprika, garlic powder, salt, black pepper, and cayenne pepper in the third bowl.
3. Bread the chicken cutlets in this order: First, dip them into the flour, coating both sides. Then, dip into the egg mixture. Finally, coat them in the panko mixture, gently pressing the breading into the chicken to help it adhere. Drizzle the cutlets with the oil.
4. To prep the pickles:
5. Pat the pickles dry with a paper towel.
6. In a small shallow bowl, whisk the egg. Add the panko to a second shallow bowl.
7. Dip the pickles in the egg, then the panko. Mist both sides of the pickles with cooking spray.
8. To cook the chicken and pickles:
9. Install a crisper plate in each of the two baskets. Place the chicken in the Zone 1 basket and insert the basket in the unit. Place the pickles in the Zone 2 basket and insert the basket in the unit.
10. Select Zone 1, select AIR FRY, set the temperature to 390°F, and set the time to 18 minutes.
11. Select Zone 2, select AIR FRY, set the temperature to 400°F, and set the time to 15 minutes. Select SMART FINISH.
12. Press START/PAUSE to begin cooking.
13. When both timers read 10 minutes, press START/PAUSE. Remove the Zone 1 basket and use silicone-tipped tongs to flip the chicken. Reinsert the basket. Remove the Zone 2 basket and shake to redistribute the pickles. Reinsert the basket and press START/PAUSE to resume cooking.
14. When cooking is complete, the breading will be crisp and golden brown and the chicken cooked through . Place one chicken cutlet on each hamburger roll. Serve the "fried" pickles on the side with ranch dressing, if desired.

Hawaiian Chicken Bites

Servings: 4
Cooking Time: 15 Minutes
Ingredients:
- 120 ml pineapple juice
- 2 tablespoons apple cider vinegar
- ½ tablespoon minced ginger
- 120 g ketchup
- 2 garlic cloves, minced
- 110 g brown sugar
- 2 tablespoons sherry
- 120 ml soy sauce
- 4 chicken breasts, cubed
- Cooking spray

Directions:
1. Combine the pineapple juice, cider vinegar, ginger, ketchup, garlic, and sugar in a saucepan. Stir to mix well. Heat over low heat for 5 minutes or until thickened. Fold in the sherry and soy sauce.
2. Dunk the chicken cubes in the mixture. Press to submerge. Wrap the bowl in plastic and refrigerate to marinate for at least an hour.
3. Preheat the air fryer to 180°C. Spritz the two air fryer drawers with cooking spray.
4. Remove the chicken cubes from the marinade. Shake the excess off and put in the preheated air fryer. Spritz with cooking spray.
5. Air fry for 15 minutes or until the chicken cubes are glazed and well browned. Shake the drawer at least three times during the frying.
6. Serve immediately.

Beef, Pork, And Lamb Recipes

Sausage Meatballs
Servings: 24
Cooking Time: 30 Minutes
Ingredients:
- 1 egg, lightly beaten
- 900g pork sausage
- 29g breadcrumbs
- 100g pimientos, drained & diced
- 1 tsp curry powder
- 1 tbsp garlic, minced
- 30ml olive oil
- 1 tbsp fresh rosemary, minced
- 25g parsley, minced
- Pepper
- Salt

Directions:
1. In a bowl, add pork sausage and remaining ingredients and mix until well combined.
2. Insert a crisper plate in the Instant air fryer baskets.
3. Make small balls from the meat mixture and place them in both baskets.
4. Select zone 1 then select "air fry" mode and set the temperature to 390 degrees F for 10 minutes. Press "match" to match zone 2 settings to zone 1. Press "start/stop" to begin.

Bacon-wrapped Filet Mignon
Servings: 4
Cooking Time: 15 Minutes
Ingredients:
- 4 bacon slices
- 4 (4-ounce) filet mignon
- Salt and ground black pepper, as required
- Olive oil cooking spray

Directions:
1. Wrap 1 bacon slice around each filet mignon and secure with toothpicks.
2. Spray the filet mignon with cooking spray evenly. Season the filets with salt and black pepper lightly.
3. Grease each basket of "Zone 1" and "Zone 2" of Instant 2-Basket Air Fryer.
4. Press "Zone 1" and "Zone 2" and then rotate the knob for each zone to select "Air Fry".
5. Set the temperature to 400 degrees F/ 200 degrees C for both zones and then set the time for 5 minutes to preheat.
6. After preheating, arrange 2 filets into the basket of each zone.
7. Slide each basket into Air Fryer and set the time for 15 minutes.
8. While cooking, flip the filets once halfway through.
9. After cooking time is completed, remove the filets from Air Fryer and serve hot.

Minute Steak Roll-ups
Servings: 4
Cooking Time: 8 To 10 Minutes
Ingredients:
- 4 minute steaks (170 g each)
- 1 (450 g) bottle Italian dressing
- 1 teaspoon salt
- ½ teaspoon freshly ground black pepper
- 120 ml finely chopped brown onion
- 120 ml finely chopped green pepper
- 120 ml finely chopped mushrooms
- 1 to 2 tablespoons oil

Directions:
1. In a large resealable bag or airtight storage container, combine the steaks and Italian dressing. Seal the bag and refrigerate to marinate for 2 hours.
2. Remove the steaks from the marinade and place them on a cutting board. Discard the marinade. Evenly season the steaks with salt and pepper.
3. In a small bowl, stir together the onion, pepper, and mushrooms. Sprinkle the onion mixture evenly over the steaks. Roll up the steaks, jelly roll-style, and secure with toothpicks.
4. Preheat the air fryer to 204ºC.
5. Place the steaks in the two air fryer drawers.
6. Cook for 4 minutes. Flip the steaks and spritz them with oil. Cook for 4 to 6 minutes more until the internal temperature reaches 64ºC. Let rest for 5 minutes before serving.

Tasty Lamb Patties

Servings: 8
Cooking Time: 12 Minutes
Ingredients:
- 900g ground lamb
- 1 tbsp ground coriander
- 4g fresh parsley, chopped
- 1 tsp garlic, minced
- ½ tsp cinnamon
- 1 tsp paprika
- 1 tbsp ground cumin
- Pepper
- Salt

Directions:
1. Add ground meat and remaining ingredients into a bowl and mix until well combined.
2. Insert a crisper plate in the Instant air fryer baskets.
3. Make patties from the meat mixture and place in both baskets.
4. Select zone 1, then select "air fry" mode and set the temperature to 390 degrees F for 12 minutes. Press "match" to match zone 2 settings to zone 1. Press "start/stop" to begin. Turn halfway through.

Goat Cheese-stuffed Bavette Steak

Servings: 6
Cooking Time: 14 Minutes
Ingredients:
- 450 g bavette or skirt steak
- 1 tablespoon avocado oil
- ½ teaspoon sea salt
- ½ teaspoon garlic powder
- ¼ teaspoon freshly ground black pepper
- 60 g goat cheese, crumbled
- 235 ml baby spinach, chopped

Directions:
1. Place the steak in a large zip-top bag or between two pieces of plastic wrap. Using a meat mallet or heavy-bottomed skillet, pound the steak to an even ¼-inch thickness.
2. Brush both sides of the steak with the avocado oil.
3. Mix the salt, garlic powder, and pepper in a small dish. Sprinkle this mixture over both sides of the steak.
4. Sprinkle the goat cheese over top, and top that with the spinach.
5. Starting at one of the long sides, roll the steak up tightly. Tie the rolled steak with kitchen string at 3-inch intervals.
6. Set the zone 1 air fryer drawer to 204°C. Place the steak roll-up in the zone 1 air fryer drawer. Air fry for 7 minutes. Flip the steak and cook for an additional 7 minutes, until an instant-read thermometer reads 49°C for medium-rare.

Bbq Pork Spare Ribs

Servings: 8
Cooking Time: 30 Minutes
Ingredients:
- ½ cup honey, divided
- 1½ cups BBQ sauce
- 4 tablespoons tomato ketchup
- 2 tablespoons Worcestershire sauce
- 2 tablespoons low-sodium soy sauce
- 1 teaspoon garlic powder
- Freshly ground white pepper, as required
- 3½ pounds pork ribs

Directions:
1. In a bowl, mix together 6 tablespoons of honey and the remaining ingredients except pork ribs.
2. Add the pork ribs and coat with the mixture generously.
3. Refrigerate to marinate for about 20 minutes.
4. Grease each basket of "Zone 1" and "Zone 2" of Instant 2-Basket Air Fryer.
5. Press "Zone 1" and "Zone 2" and then rotate the knob for each zone to select "Air Fry".
6. Set the temperature to 355 degrees F/ 180 degrees C for both zones and then set the time for 5 minutes to preheat.
7. After preheating, arrange the ribs into the basket of each zone.
8. Slide each basket into Air Fryer and set the time for 26 minutes.
9. While cooking, flip the ribs once halfway through.
10. After cooking time is completed, remove the ribs from Air Fryer and place onto serving plates.
11. Drizzle with the remaining honey and serve immediately.

Sausage-stuffed Peppers

Servings: 6
Cooking Time: 28 To 30 Minutes
Ingredients:
- Avocado oil spray
- 230 g Italian-seasoned sausage, casings removed
- 120 ml chopped mushrooms
- 60 ml diced onion
- 1 teaspoon Italian seasoning
- Sea salt and freshly ground black pepper, to taste
- 235 ml keto-friendly marinara sauce
- 3 peppers, halved and seeded
- 85 g low-moisture Mozzarella or other melting cheese, shredded

Directions:
1. Spray a large skillet with oil and place it over medium-high heat. Add the sausage and cook for 5 minutes, breaking up the meat with a wooden spoon. Add the mushrooms, onion, and Italian seasoning, and season with salt and pepper. Cook for 5 minutes more. Stir in the marinara sauce and cook until heated through.
2. Scoop the sausage filling into the pepper halves.
3. Set the air fryer to 176°C. Arrange the peppers in a single layer in the two air fryer drawers. Air fry for 15 minutes.
4. Top the stuffed peppers with the cheese and air fry for 3 to 5 minutes more, until the cheese is melted and the peppers are tender.

Air Fried Lamb Chops

Servings: 4
Cooking Time: 10 Minutes
Ingredients:
- 700g lamb chops
- ½ teaspoon oregano
- 3 tablespoons parsley, minced
- ½ teaspoon black pepper
- 3 cloves garlic minced
- 2 tablespoons lemon juice
- 2 tablespoons olive oil
- Salt to taste

Directions:
1. Pat dry the chops and mix with lemon juice and the rest of the ingredients.
2. Place these chops in the air fryer baskets.
3. Return the air fryer basket 1 to Zone 1, and basket 2 to Zone 2 of the Instant 2-Basket Air Fryer.
4. Choose the "Air Fry" mode for Zone 1and set the temperature to 400 degrees F and 10 minutes of cooking time.
5. Select the "MATCH COOK" option to copy the settings for Zone 2.
6. Initiate cooking by pressing the START/PAUSE BUTTON.
7. Flip the pork chops once cooked halfway through.
8. Serve warm.

Sumptuous Pizza Tortilla Rolls

Servings: 4
Cooking Time: 6 Minutes
Ingredients:
- 1 teaspoon butter
- ½ medium onion, slivered
- ½ red or green pepper, julienned
- 110 g fresh white mushrooms, chopped
- 120 ml pizza sauce
- 8 flour tortillas
- 8 thin slices wafer-thinham
- 24 pepperoni slices
- 235 ml shredded Mozzarella cheese
- Cooking spray

Directions:
1. Preheat the air fryer to 200°C.
2. Put butter, onions, pepper, and mushrooms in a baking pan. Bake in the preheated air fryer for 3 minutes. Stir and cook 3 to 4 minutes longer until just crisp and tender. Remove pan and set aside.
3. To assemble rolls, spread about 2 teaspoons of pizza sauce on one half of each tortilla. Top with a slice of ham and 3 slices of pepperoni. Divide sautéed vegetables among tortillas and top with cheese.
4. Roll up tortillas, secure with toothpicks if needed, and spray with oil.
5. Put the rolls in the two air fryer drawers and air fry for 4 minutes. Turn and air fry 4 minutes, until heated through and lightly browned.
6. Serve immediately.

Simple Beef Sirloin Roast

Servings: 16
Cooking Time: 50 Minutes
Ingredients:
- 2 (2½-pound) sirloin roast
- Salt and ground black pepper, as required

Directions:
1. Grease each basket of "Zone 1" and "Zone 2" of Instant 2-Basket Air Fryer.
2. Press "Zone 1" and "Zone 2" and then rotate the knob for each zone to select "Roast".
3. Set the temperature to 350 degrees F/ 175 degrees C for both zones and then set the time for 5 minutes to preheat.
4. Rub ach roast with salt and black pepper generously.
5. After preheating, arrange 1 roast into the basket of each zone.
6. Slide each basket into Air Fryer and set the time for 50 minutes.
7. After cooking time is completed, remove each roast from Air Fryer and place onto a platter for about 10 minutes before slicing.
8. With a sharp knife, cut each roast into desired-sized slices and serve.

Curry-crusted Lamb Chops With Baked Brown Sugar Acorn Squash

Servings:4
Cooking Time: 20 Minutes
Ingredients:
- FOR THE LAMB CHOPS
- 4 lamb loin chops (4 ounces each)
- 1 tablespoon olive oil
- 2 teaspoons curry powder
- ¼ teaspoon kosher salt
- FOR THE ACORN SQUASH
- 2 small acorn squash
- 4 teaspoons dark brown sugar
- 2 teaspoons salted butter
- ⅛ teaspoon kosher salt

Directions:
1. To prep the lamb chops: Brush both sides of the lamb chops with the oil and season with the curry powder and salt.
2. To prep the acorn squash: Cut the squash in half through the stem end and remove the seeds. Place 1 teaspoon of brown sugar and ½ teaspoon of butter into the well of each squash half.
3. To cook the lamb and squash: Install a crisper plate in each of the two baskets. Place the lamb chops in the Zone 1 basket and insert the basket in the unit. Place the squash cut-side up in the Zone 2 basket and insert the basket in the unit.
4. Select Zone 1, select AIR FRY, set the temperature to 400°F, and set the timer to 15 minutes.
5. Select Zone 2, select BAKE, set the temperature to 400°F, and set the time to 20 minutes. Select SMART FINISH.
6. Press START/PAUSE to begin cooking.
7. When both timers read 5 minutes, press START/PAUSE. Remove the Zone 1 basket and use a pair of silicone-tipped tongs to flip the lamb chops. Reinsert the basket in the unit. Remove the Zone 2 basket and spoon the melted butter and sugar over the top edges of the squash. Reinsert the basket and press START/PAUSE to resume cooking.
8. When cooking is complete, the lamb should be cooked to your liking and the squash soft when pierced with a fork.
9. Remove the lamb chops from the basket and let rest for 5 minutes. Season the acorn squash with salt before serving.

Nutrition:
- (Per serving) Calories: 328; Total fat: 19g; Saturated fat: 7.5g; Carbohydrates: 23g; Fiber: 3g; Protein: 16g; Sodium: 172mg

Mustard Pork Chops

Servings: 4
Cooking Time: 15 Minutes
Ingredients:
- 450g pork chops, boneless
- 55g brown mustard
- 85g honey
- 57g mayonnaise
- 34g BBQ sauce
- Pepper
- Salt

Directions:
1. Coat pork chops with mustard, honey, mayonnaise, BBQ sauce, pepper, and salt in a bowl. Cover and place the bowl in the refrigerator for 1 hour.
2. Insert a crisper plate in the Instant air fryer baskets.
3. Place the marinated pork chops in both baskets.
4. Select zone 1, then select "bake" mode and set the temperature to 380 degrees F for 15 minutes. Press "match" and then press "start/stop" to begin. Turn halfway through.

Steak And Asparagus Bundles

Servings: 6
Cooking Time: 10 Minutes
Ingredients:
- 907g flank steak, cut into 6 pieces
- Salt and black pepper, to taste
- ½ cup tamari sauce
- 2 cloves garlic, crushed
- 455g asparagus, trimmed
- 3 capsicums, sliced
- ¼ cup balsamic vinegar
- 79 ml beef broth
- 2 tablespoons unsalted butter
- Olive oil spray

Directions:
1. Mix steaks with black pepper, tamari sauce, and garlic in a Ziplock bag.
2. Seal the bag, shake well and refrigerate for 1 hour.
3. Place the steaks on the working surface and top each with asparagus and capsicums.
4. Roll the steaks and secure them with toothpicks.
5. Place these rolls in the air fryer baskets.
6. Return the air fryer basket 1 to Zone 1, and basket 2 to Zone 2 of the Instant 2-Basket Air Fryer.
7. Choose the "Air Fry" mode for Zone 1 and set the temperature to 400 degrees F and 10 minutes of cooking time.
8. Select the "MATCH COOK" option to copy the settings for Zone 2.
9. Initiate cooking by pressing the START/PAUSE BUTTON.
10. Meanwhile, cook broth with butter and vinegar in a saucepan.
11. Cook this mixture until reduced by half and adjust seasoning with black pepper and salt.
12. Serve the steak rolls with the prepared sauce.

Pigs In A Blanket With Spinach-artichoke Stuffed Mushrooms

Servings: 4
Cooking Time: 15 Minutes
Ingredients:
- FOR THE PIGS IN A BLANKET
- Half an 8-ounce tube refrigerated crescent roll dough
- 4 hot dogs
- ½ teaspoon everything bagel seasoning (optional)
- FOR THE STUFFED MUSHROOMS
- 1 cup frozen chopped spinach, thawed and drained
- 1 (14-ounce) can artichoke hearts, drained and chopped
- 2 ounces (¼ cup) cream cheese, at room temperature
- ¼ cup grated Parmesan cheese
- ½ teaspoon garlic powder
- 1 (8-ounce) package whole cremini mushrooms, stems removed

Directions:
1. To prep the pigs in a blanket: Unroll the crescent roll dough. It will be scored into 4 triangular pieces, but leave them in place and pinch together at the seams to form 1 large square of dough. Cut the dough into 4 strips.
2. Wrap one strip of dough around each hot dog, starting with a short end of the strips and wrapping in a spiral motion around the hot dog. If desired, sprinkle each pig in a blanket with everything bagel seasoning.
3. To prep the stuffed mushrooms: In a medium bowl, combine the spinach, artichoke hearts, cream cheese, Parmesan, and garlic powder. Stuff about 1 tablespoon of filling into each mushroom cap.
4. To cook the pigs in a blanket and mushrooms: Install a crisper plate in each of the two baskets. Place the pigs in a blanket in the Zone 1 basket and insert the basket in the unit. Place the mushrooms in the Zone 2 basket and insert the basket in the unit.
5. Select Zone 1, select AIR FRY, set the temperature to 370°F, and set the time to 8 minutes.
6. Select Zone 2, select BAKE, set the temperature to 370°F, and set the time to 15 minutes. Select SMART FINISH.
7. Press START/PAUSE to begin cooking.
8. When cooking is complete, the crescent roll dough should be cooked through and golden brown, and the mushrooms should be tender.

Nutrition:
- (Per serving) Calories: 371; Total fat: 25g; Saturated fat: 11g; Carbohydrates: 22g; Fiber: 2.5g; Protein: 14g; Sodium: 1,059mg

Mojito Lamb Chops

Servings: 2
Cooking Time: 5 Minutes
Ingredients:
- Marinade:
- 2 teaspoons grated lime zest
- 120 ml lime juice
- 60 ml avocado oil
- 60 ml chopped fresh mint leaves
- 4 cloves garlic, roughly chopped
- 2 teaspoons fine sea salt
- ½ teaspoon ground black pepper
- 4 (1-inch-thick) lamb chops
- Sprigs of fresh mint, for garnish (optional)
- Lime slices, for serving (optional)

Directions:
1. Make the marinade: Place all the ingredients for the marinade in a food processor or blender and purée until mostly smooth with a few small chunks. Transfer half of the marinade to a shallow dish and set the other half aside for serving. Add the lamb to the shallow dish, cover, and place in the refrigerator to marinate for at least 2 hours or overnight. 2. Spray the two air fryer drawers with avocado oil. Preheat the air fryer to 200°C. 3. Remove the chops from the marinade and place them in the two air fryer drawers. Air fry for 5 minutes, or until the internal temperature reaches 64°C for medium doneness. 4. Allow the chops to rest for 10 minutes before serving with the rest of the marinade as a sauce. Garnish with fresh mint leaves and serve with lime slices, if desired. Best served fresh.

Beef And Bean Taquitos With Mexican Rice

Servings:4
Cooking Time: 15 Minutes
Ingredients:
- FOR THE TAQUITOS
- ½ pound ground beef (85 percent lean)
- 1 tablespoon taco seasoning
- 8 (6-inch) soft white corn tortillas
- Nonstick cooking spray
- ¾ cup canned refried beans
- ½ cup shredded Mexican blend cheese (optional)
- FOR THE MEXICAN RICE
- 1 cup dried instant white rice (not microwavable)
- 1½ cups chicken broth
- ¼ cup jarred salsa
- 2 tablespoons canned tomato sauce
- 1 tablespoon vegetable oil
- ½ teaspoon kosher salt

Directions:
1. To prep the taquitos: In a large bowl, mix the ground beef and taco seasoning until well combined.
2. Mist both sides of each tortilla lightly with cooking spray.
3. To prep the Mexican rice: In the Zone 2 basket, combine the rice, broth, salsa, tomato sauce, oil, and salt. Stir well to ensure all of the rice is submerged in the liquid.
4. To cook the taquitos and rice: Install a crisper plate in the Zone 1 basket. Place the seasoned beef in the basket and insert the basket in the unit. Insert the Zone 2 basket in the unit.
5. Select Zone 1, select AIR FRY, set the temperature to 390°F, and set the time to 15 minutes.
6. Select Zone 2, select BAKE, set the temperature to 350°F, and set the time to 10 minutes. Select SMART FINISH.
7. Press START/PAUSE to begin cooking.
8. When the Zone 1 timer reads 10 minutes, press START/PAUSE. Remove the basket and transfer the beef to a medium bowl. Add the refried beans and cheese (if using) and combine well. Spoon 2 tablespoons of the filling onto each tortilla and roll tightly. Place the taquitos in the Zone 1 basket seam-side down. Reinsert the basket in the unit and press START/PAUSE to resume cooking.
9. When cooking is complete, the taquitos should be crisp and golden brown and the rice cooked through. Serve hot.

Nutrition:
- (Per serving) Calories: 431; Total fat: 18g; Saturated fat: 4g; Carbohydrates: 52g; Fiber: 5.5g; Protein: 18g; Sodium: 923mg

Hot Dogs Wrapped In Bacon

Servings: 2
Cooking Time: 20 Minutes
Ingredients:
- 2 bacon strips
- 2 hot dogs
- Salt and black pepper, to taste

Directions:
1. Wrap each hot dog with bacon strip and season with salt and black pepper.
2. Grease each basket of "Zone 1" and "Zone 2" of Instant 2-Basket Air Fryer.
3. Press "Zone 1" and "Zone 2" and then rotate the knob for each zone to select "Air Fry".
4. Set the temperature to 400 degrees F/ 200 degrees C for both zones and then set the time for 5 minutes to preheat.
5. After preheating, arrange bacon wrapped hot dogs into the basket of each zone.
6. Slide each basket into Air Fryer and set the time for 15 minutes.
7. While cooking, flip the hot dogs once halfway through.
8. After cooking time is completed, remove the filets from Air Fryer and serve hot.

Garlic Butter Steaks

Servings: 2
Cooking Time: 25 Minutes
Ingredients:
- 2 (6 ounces each) sirloin steaks or ribeyes
- 2 tablespoons unsalted butter
- 1 clove garlic, crushed
- ½ teaspoon dried parsley
- ½ teaspoon dried rosemary
- Salt and pepper, to taste

Directions:
1. Season the steaks with salt and pepper and set them to rest for about 2 hours before cooking.
2. Put the butter in a bowl. Add the garlic, parsley, and rosemary. Allow the butter to soften.
3. Whip together with a fork or spoon once the butter has softened.
4. When you're ready to cook, install a crisper plate in both drawers. Place the sirloin steaks in a single layer in each drawer. Insert the drawers into the unit.
5. Select zone 1, select AIR FRY, set temperature to 360 degrees F/ 180 degrees C, and set time to 10 minutes. Select MATCH to match zone 2 settings to zone 1. Select START/STOP to begin.
6. Once done, serve with the garlic butter.

Nutrition:
- (Per serving) Calories 519 | Fat 36g | Sodium 245mg | Carbs 1g | Fiber 0g | Sugar 0g | Protein 46g

Air Fryer Meatloaves

Servings: 4
Cooking Time: 22 Minutes.
Ingredients:
- ⅓ cup milk
- 2 tablespoons basil pesto
- 1 egg, beaten
- 1 garlic clove, minced
- ¼ teaspoons black pepper
- 1 lb. ground beef
- ⅓ cup panko bread crumbs
- 8 pepperoni slices
- ½ cup marinara sauce, warmed
- 1 tablespoon fresh basil, chopped

Directions:
1. Mix pesto, milk, egg, garlic, and black pepper in a medium-sized bowl.
2. Stir in ground beef and bread crumbs, then mix.
3. Make the 4 small-sized loaves with this mixture and top them with 2 pepperoni slices.
4. Press the slices into the meatloaves.
5. Place the meatloaves in the two crisper plates.
6. Return the crisper plate to the Instant Dual Zone Air Fryer.
7. Choose the Air Fry mode for Zone 1 and set the temperature to 390 degrees F and the time to 22 minutes.
8. Select the "MATCH" button to copy the settings for Zone 2.
9. Initiate cooking by pressing the START/STOP button.
10. Top them with marinara sauce and basil to serve.
11. Serve warm.

Nutrition:
- (Per serving) Calories 316 | Fat 12.2g |Sodium 587mg | Carbs 12.2g | Fiber 1g | Sugar 1.8g | Protein 25.8g

Honey-baked Pork Loin

Servings: 6
Cooking Time: 22 To 25 Minutes
Ingredients:
- 60 ml honey
- 60 ml freshly squeezed lemon juice
- 2 tablespoons soy sauce
- 1 teaspoon garlic powder
- 1 (900 g) pork loin
- 2 tablespoons vegetable oil

Directions:
1. In a medium bowl, whisk together the honey, lemon juice, soy sauce, and garlic powder. Reserve half of the mixture for basting during cooking.
2. Cut 5 slits in the pork loin and transfer it to a resealable bag. Add the remaining honey mixture. Seal the bag and refrigerate to marinate for at least 2 hours.
3. Preheat the air fryer to 204°C. Line the two air fryer drawers with parchment paper.
4. Remove the pork from the marinade, and place it on the parchment. Spritz with oil, then baste with the reserved marinade.
5. Cook for 15 minutes. Flip the pork, baste with more marinade and spritz with oil again. Cook for 7 to 10 minutes more until the internal temperature reaches 64°C. Let rest for 5 minutes before serving.

Stuffed Beef Fillet With Feta Cheese

Servings: 4
Cooking Time: 10 Minutes
Ingredients:
- 680 g beef fillet, pounded to ¼ inch thick
- 3 teaspoons sea salt
- 1 teaspoon ground black pepper
- 60 g creamy goat cheese
- 120 ml crumbled feta cheese
- 60 ml finely chopped onions
- 2 cloves garlic, minced
- Cooking spray

Directions:
1. Preheat the air fryer to 204°C. Spritz the two air fryer drawers with cooking spray. 2. Unfold the beef on a clean work surface. Rub the salt and pepper all over the beef to season. 3. Make the filling for the stuffed beef fillet: Combine the goat cheese, feta, onions, and garlic in a medium bowl. Stir until well blended. 4. Spoon the mixture in the center of the fillet. Roll the fillet up tightly like rolling a burrito and use some kitchen twine to tie the fillet. 5. Arrange the fillet in the two air fryer drawers and air fry for 10 minutes, flipping the fillet halfway through to ensure even cooking, or until an instant-read thermometer inserted in the center of the fillet registers 57°C for medium-rare. 6. Transfer to a platter and serve immediately.

Blue Cheese Steak Salad

Servings: 4
Cooking Time: 22 Minutes
Ingredients:
- 2 tablespoons balsamic vinegar
- 2 tablespoons red wine vinegar
- 1 tablespoon Dijon mustard
- 1 tablespoon granulated sweetener
- 1 teaspoon minced garlic
- Sea salt and freshly ground black pepper, to taste
- 180 ml extra-virgin olive oil
- 450 g boneless rump steak
- Avocado oil spray
- 1 small red onion, cut into ¼-inch-thick rounds
- 170 g baby spinach
- 120 ml cherry tomatoes, halved
- 85 g blue cheese, crumbled

Directions:
1. In a blender, combine the balsamic vinegar, red wine vinegar, Dijon mustard, sweetener, and garlic. Season with salt and pepper and process until smooth. With the blender running, drizzle in the olive oil. Process until well combined. Transfer to a jar with a tight-fitting lid, and refrigerate until ready to serve.
2. Season the steak with salt and pepper and let sit at room temperature for at least 45 minutes, time permitting.
3. Set the zone 1 air fryer drawer to 204°C. Spray the steak with oil and place it in the zone 1 air fryer drawer. Spray the onion slices with oil and place them in the zone 2 air fryer drawer.
4. In zone 1, air fry for 6 minutes. Flip the steak and spray it with more oil. Air fry for 6 minutes more for medium-rare or until the steak is done to your liking.
5. In zone 2, cook at 204°C for 5 minutes. Flip the onion slices and spray them with more oil. Air fry for 5 minutes more.
6. Transfer the steak to a plate, tent with a piece of aluminum foil, and allow it to rest. Slice the steak diagonally into thin strips. Place the spinach, cherry tomatoes, onion slices, and steak in a large bowl. Toss with the desired amount of dressing. Sprinkle with crumbled blue cheese and serve.

Gochujang Brisket

Servings: 6
Cooking Time: 55 Minutes.
Ingredients:
- ½ tablespoons sweet paprika
- ½ teaspoon toasted sesame oil
- 2 lbs. beef brisket, cut into 4 pieces
- Salt, to taste
- ⅛ cup Gochujang, Korean chili paste
- Black pepper, to taste
- 1 small onion, diced
- 2 garlic cloves, minced
- 1 teaspoon Asian fish sauce
- 1 ½ tablespoons peanut oil, as needed
- ½ tablespoon fresh ginger, grated
- ¼ teaspoon red chili flakes
- ½ cup of water
- 1 tablespoon ketchup
- 1 tablespoon soy sauce

Directions:
1. Thoroughly rub the beef brisket with olive oil, paprika, chili flakes, black pepper, and salt.
2. Cut the brisket in half, then divide the beef in the two crisper plate.
3. Return the crisper plate to the Instant Dual Zone Air Fryer.
4. Choose the Air Fry mode for Zone 1 and set the temperature to 390 degrees F and the time to 35 minutes.
5. Select the "MATCH" button to copy the settings for Zone 2.
6. Initiate cooking by pressing the START/STOP button.
7. Flip the brisket halfway through, and resume cooking.
8. Meanwhile, heat oil in a skillet and add ginger, onion, and garlic.
9. Sauté for 5 minutes, then add all the remaining ingredients.
10. Cook the mixture for 15 minutes approximately until well thoroughly mixed.
11. Serve the brisket with this sauce on top.

Nutrition:
- (Per serving) Calories 374 | Fat 25g |Sodium 275mg | Carbs 7.3g | Fiber 0g | Sugar 6g | Protein 12.3g

Simple Strip Steak

Servings: 4
Cooking Time: 10 Minutes
Ingredients:
- 2 (9½-ounce) New York strip steaks
- Salt and ground black pepper, as required
- 3 teaspoons olive oil

Directions:
1. Grease each basket of "Zone 1" and "Zone 2" of Instant 2-Basket Air Fryer.
2. Press "Zone 1" and "Zone 2" and then rotate the knob for each zone to select "Air Fry".
3. Set the temperature to 400 degrees F/ 200 degrees C for both zones and then set the time for 5 minutes to preheat.
4. Coat the steaks with oil and then sprinkle with salt and black pepper evenly.
5. After preheating, arrange 1 steak into the basket of each zone.
6. Slide each basket into Air Fryer and set the time for 10 minutes.
7. While cooking, flip the steak once halfway through.
8. After cooking time is completed, remove the steaks from Air Fryer and place onto a platter for about 10 minutes.
9. Cut each steak into desired size slices and serve immediately.

Roasted Beef

Servings: 8
Cooking Time: 50 Minutes
Ingredients:
- 1 (1-pound) beef roast
- Salt and ground black pepper, as required

Directions:
1. Grease each basket of "Zone 1" and "Zone 2" of Instant 2-Basket Air Fryer.
2. Press "Zone 1" and "Zone 2" and then rotate the knob for each zone to select "Roast".
3. Set the temperature to 350 degrees F/ 175 degrees C for both zones and then set the time for 5 minutes to preheat.
4. Rub ach roast with salt and black pepper generously.
5. After preheating, arrange the roast into the basket of each zone.
6. Slide each basket into Air Fryer and set the time for 50 minutes.
7. After cooking time is completed, remove each roast from Air Fryer and place onto a platter for about 10 minutes before slicing.
8. With a sharp knife, cut each roast into desired-sized slices and serve.

Mustard Rubbed Lamb Chops

Servings: 4
Cooking Time: 31 Minutes.
Ingredients:
- 1 teaspoon Dijon mustard
- 1 teaspoon olive oil
- ½ teaspoon soy sauce
- ½ teaspoon garlic, minced
- ½ teaspoon cumin powder
- ½ teaspoon cayenne pepper
- ½ teaspoon Italian spice blend
- ⅛ teaspoon salt
- 4 pieces of lamb chops

Directions:
1. Mix Dijon mustard, soy sauce, olive oil, garlic, cumin powder, cayenne pepper, Italian spice blend, and salt in a medium bowl and mix well.
2. Place lamb chops into a Ziploc bag and pour in the marinade.
3. Press the air out of the bag and seal tightly.
4. Press the marinade around the lamb chops to coat.
5. Keep then in the fridge and marinate for at least 30 minutes, up to overnight.
6. Place 2 chops in each of the crisper plate and spray them with cooking oil.
7. Return the crisper plate to the Instant Dual Zone Air Fryer.
8. Select the Roast mode for Zone 1 and set the temperature to 350 degrees F and the time to 27 minutes.
9. Select the "MATCH" button to copy the settings for Zone 2.
10. Initiate cooking by pressing the START/STOP button.
11. Flip the chops once cooked halfway through, and resume cooking.
12. Switch the Roast mode to Max Crisp mode and cook for 5 minutes.
13. Serve warm.

Nutrition:
- (Per serving) Calories 264 | Fat 17g |Sodium 129mg | Carbs 0.9g | Fiber 0.3g | Sugar 0g | Protein 27g

Garlic-rosemary Pork Loin With Scalloped Potatoes And Cauliflower

Servings:6
Cooking Time: 50 Minutes
Ingredients:
- FOR THE PORK LOIN
- 2 pounds pork loin roast
- 2 tablespoons vegetable oil
- 2 teaspoons dried thyme
- 2 teaspoons dried crushed rosemary
- 1 teaspoon minced garlic
- ¾ teaspoon kosher salt
- FOR THE SCALLOPED POTATOES AND CAULIFLOWER
- 1 teaspoon vegetable oil
- ¾ pound Yukon Gold potatoes, peeled and very thinly sliced
- 1½ cups cauliflower florets
- ¼ teaspoon kosher salt
- ¼ teaspoon freshly ground black pepper
- 1 tablespoon very cold unsalted butter, grated
- 3 tablespoons all-purpose flour
- 1 cup whole milk
- 1 cup shredded Gruyère cheese

Directions:
1. To prep the pork loin: Coat the pork with the oil. Season with thyme, rosemary, garlic, and salt.
2. To prep the potatoes and cauliflower: Brush the bottom and sides of the Zone 2 basket with the oil. Add one-third of the potatoes to the bottom of the basket and arrange in a single layer. Top with ½ cup of cauliflower florets. Sprinkle a third of the salt and black pepper on top. Scatter one-third of the butter on top and sprinkle on 1 tablespoon of flour. Repeat this step twice more for a total of three layers.
3. Pour the milk over the layered potatoes and cauliflower; it should just cover the top layer. Top with the Gruyère.
4. To cook the pork and scalloped vegetables: Install a crisper plate in the Zone 1 basket. Place the pork loin in the basket and insert the basket in the unit. Insert the Zone 2 basket in the unit.
5. Select Zone 1, select AIR FRY, set the temperature to 390°F, and set the time to 50 minutes.
6. Select Zone 2, select BAKE, set the temperature to 350°F, and set the time to 45 minutes. Select SMART FINISH.
7. Press START/PAUSE to begin cooking.
8. When cooking is complete, the pork will be cooked through (an instant-read thermometer should read 145°F) and the potatoes and cauliflower will be tender.
9. Let the pork rest for at least 15 minutes before slicing and serving with the scalloped vegetables.

Nutrition:
- (Per serving) Calories: 439; Total fat: 25g; Saturated fat: 10g; Carbohydrates: 17g; Fiber: 1.5g; Protein: 37g; Sodium: 431mg

Cilantro Lime Steak

Servings: 4
Cooking Time: 10 Minutes
Ingredients:
- 450g flank steak, sliced
- 1 tsp cumin
- 1 tsp olive oil
- 4 tsp soy sauce
- 12g cilantro, chopped
- ¼ tsp cayenne
- 45ml lime juice
- 2 tsp chilli powder
- ¼ tsp salt

Directions:
1. Add the sliced steak pieces and the remaining ingredients into a zip-lock bag. Seal the bag and place in the refrigerator for 2 hours.
2. Insert a crisper plate in the Instant air fryer baskets.
3. Place the marinated steak pieces in both baskets.
4. Select zone 1, then select "air fry" mode and set the temperature to 380 degrees F for 10 minutes. Press "match" to match zone 2 settings to zone 1. Press "start/stop" to begin.

Bacon Wrapped Pork Tenderloin

Servings: 2
Cooking Time: 20 Minutes
Ingredients:
- ½ teaspoon salt
- ¼ teaspoon black pepper
- 1 pork tenderloin
- 6 center cut strips bacon
- cooking string

Directions:
1. Cut two bacon strips in half and place them on the working surface.
2. Place the other bacon strips on top and lay the tenderloin over the bacon strip.
3. Wrap the bacon around the tenderloin and tie the roast with a kitchen string.
4. Place the roast in the first air fryer basket.
5. Return the air fryer basket 1 to Zone 1, and basket 2 to Zone 2 of the Instant 2-Basket Air Fryer.
6. Choose the "Air Fry" mode for Zone 1 and set the temperature to 400 degrees F and 20 minutes of cooking time.
7. Initiate cooking by pressing the START/PAUSE BUTTON.
8. Slice and serve warm.

Asian Pork Skewers

Servings: 4
Cooking Time: 30 Minutes
Ingredients:
- 450g pork shoulder, sliced
- 30g ginger, peeled and crushed
- ½ tablespoon crushed garlic
- 67½ml soy sauce
- 22½ml honey
- 22½ml rice vinegar
- 10ml toasted sesame oil
- 8 skewers

Directions:
1. Pound the pork slices with a mallet.
2. Mix ginger, garlic, soy sauce, honey, rice vinegar, and sesame oil in a bowl.
3. Add pork slices to the marinade and mix well to coat.
4. Cover and marinate the pork for 30 minutes.
5. Thread the pork on the wooden skewers and place them in the air fryer baskets.
6. Return the air fryer basket 1 to Zone 1, and basket 2 to Zone 2 of the Instant 2-Basket Air Fryer.
7. Choose the "Air Fry" mode for Zone 1 and set the temperature to 350 degrees F and 25 minutes of cooking time.
8. Select the "MATCH COOK" option to copy the settings for Zone 2.
9. Initiate cooking by pressing the START/PAUSE BUTTON.
10. Flip the skewers once cooked halfway through.
11. Serve warm.

Easy Breaded Pork Chops

Servings: 8
Cooking Time: 20 Minutes
Ingredients:
- 1 egg
- 118ml milk
- 8 pork chops
- 1 packet ranch seasoning
- 238g breadcrumbs
- Pepper
- Salt

Directions:
1. In a small bowl, whisk the egg and milk.
2. In a separate shallow dish, mix breadcrumbs, ranch seasoning, pepper, and salt.
3. Dip each pork chop in the egg mixture, then coat with breadcrumbs.
4. Insert a crisper plate in the Instant air fryer baskets.
5. Place the coated pork chops in both baskets.
6. Select zone 1, then select air fry mode and set the temperature to 360 degrees F for 12 minutes. Press "match" to match zone 2 settings to zone 1. Press "start/stop" to begin. Turn halfway through.

Snacks And Appetizers Recipes

Beef Skewers

Servings: 6
Cooking Time: 5 Minutes
Ingredients:
- 1 beef flank steak
- 240ml rice vinegar
- 240ml soy sauce
- 55g packed brown sugar
- 2 tablespoons minced fresh gingerroot
- 6 garlic cloves, minced
- 3 teaspoons sesame oil
- 1 teaspoon hot pepper sauce
- ½ teaspoon cornflour

Directions:
1. Cut beef into ½ cm thick strips. Whisk together the following 7 ingredients in a large mixing bowl until well combined.
2. In a shallow dish, pour 1 cup of marinade. Toss in the beef and turn to coat. Refrigerate for 2-8 hours, covered. Cover and keep the remaining marinade refrigerated.
3. Beef should be drained. 12 metal or wet wooden skewers threaded with beef.
4. Press either "Zone 1" or "Zone 2" and then rotate the knob to select "Air Fry".
5. Set the temperature to 200 degrees C, and then set the time for 5 minutes to preheat.
6. After preheating, spray the basket with cooking spray and arrange skewers onto basket.
7. Slide the basket into the Air Fryer and set the time for 5 minutes.
8. After cooking time is completed, transfer them onto serving plates and serve.

Garlic Bread

Servings: 8
Cooking Time: 10 Minutes
Ingredients:
- 60g butter, softened
- 3 tablespoons grated Parmesan cheese
- 2 garlic cloves, minced
- 2 teaspoons minced fresh parsley
- 8 slices of French bread

Directions:
1. Press either "Zone 1" or "Zone 2" and then rotate the knob to select "Bake".
2. Set the temperature to 175 degrees C, and then set the time for 5 minutes to preheat.
3. After preheating, combine the first four ingredients in a small mixing bowl| spread on bread. Arrange bread slices onto basket.
4. Slide the basket into the Air Fryer and set the time for 3 minutes.
5. After cooking time is completed, transfer them onto serving plates and serve.

Cheese Drops

Servings: 8
Cooking Time: 10 Minutes
Ingredients:
- 177 ml plain flour
- ½ teaspoon rock salt
- ¼ teaspoon cayenne pepper
- ¼ teaspoon smoked paprika
- ¼ teaspoon black pepper
- Dash garlic powder (optional)
- 60 ml butter, softened
- 240 ml shredded extra mature Cheddar cheese, at room temperature
- Olive oil spray

Directions:
1. In a small bowl, combine the flour, salt, cayenne, paprika, pepper, and garlic powder, if using. 2. Using a food processor, cream the butter and cheese until smooth. Gently add the seasoned flour and process until the dough is well combined, smooth, and no longer sticky. 3. Divide the dough into 32 equal-size pieces. On a lightly floured surface, roll each piece into a small ball. 4. Spray the two air fryer baskets with oil spray. Arrange the cheese drops in the two baskets. Set the air fryer to 165°C for 10 minutes, or until drops are just starting to brown. Transfer to a wire rack. 5. Cool the cheese drops completely on the wire rack. Store in an airtight container until ready to serve, or up to 1 or 2 days.

Chicken Tenders

Servings: 3
Cooking Time: 12
Ingredients:
- 1 pound of chicken tender
- Salt and black pepper, to taste
- 1 cup Panko bread crumbs
- 2 cups Italian bread crumbs
- 1 cup parmesan cheese
- 2 eggs
- Oil spray, for greasing

Directions:
1. Sprinkle the tenders with salt and black pepper.
2. In a medium bowl mix Panko bread crumbs with Italian breadcrumbs.
3. Add salt, pepper, and parmesan cheese.
4. Crack two eggs in a bowl.
5. First, put the chicken tender in eggs.
6. Now dredge the tender in a bowl and coat the tender well with crumbs.
7. Line both of the baskets of the air fryer with parchment paper.
8. At the end spray the tenders with oil spray.
9. Divided the tenders between the baskets of Instante 2-Basket Air Fryer.
10. Set zone 1 basket to AIR FRY mode at 350 degrees F for 12 minutes.
11. Select the MATCH button for the zone 2 basket.
12. Once it's done, serve.

Nutrition:
- (Per serving) Calories558 | Fat23.8g | Sodium872 mg | Carbs 20.9g | Fiber1.7 g| Sugar2.2 g | Protein 63.5g

Kale Chips

Servings: 4
Cooking Time: 3 Minutes
Ingredients:
- 1 head fresh kale, stems and ribs removed and cut into 4cm pieces
- 1 tablespoon olive oil
- 1 teaspoon soy sauce
- ⅛ teaspoon cayenne pepper
- Pinch of freshly ground black pepper

Directions:
1. In a large bowl, add all the ingredients and mix well.
2. Grease basket of Instant 2-Basket Air Fryer.
3. Press your chosen zone - "Zone 1" or "Zone 2" and then rotate the knob to select "Air Fry".
4. Set the temperature to 200 degrees C and then set the time for 5 minutes to preheat.
5. After preheating, arrange the kale pieces into the basket of each zone.
6. Slide the basket into the Air Fryer and set the time for 3 minutes.
7. While cooking, toss the kale pieces once halfway through.
8. After cooking time is completed, remove the kale chips and baking pans from Air Fryer.
9. Place the kale chips onto a wire rack to cool for about 10 minutes before serving.

Five-ingredient Falafel With Garlic-yoghurt Sauce

Servings: 4
Cooking Time: 15 Minutes
Ingredients:
- Falafel:
- 1 (425 g) can chickpeas, drained and rinsed
- 120 ml fresh parsley
- 2 garlic cloves, minced
- ½ tablespoon ground cumin
- 1 tablespoon wholemeal flour
- Salt
- Garlic-Yoghurt Sauce:
- 240 ml non-fat plain Greek yoghurt
- 1 garlic clove, minced
- 1 tablespoon chopped fresh dill
- 2 tablespoons lemon juice

Directions:
1. Make the Falafel: Preheat the air fryer to 180°C. 2. Put the chickpeas into a food processor. Pulse until mostly chopped, then add the parsley, garlic, and cumin and pulse for another 1 to 2 minutes, or until the ingredients are combined and turning into a dough. 3. Add the flour. Pulse a few more times until combined. The dough will have texture, but the chickpeas should be pulsed into small bits. 4. Using clean hands, roll the dough into 8 balls of equal size, then pat the balls down a bit so they are about ½-thick disks. 5. Spray the zone 1 air fryer basket with olive oil cooking spray, then place the falafel patties in the basket in a single layer, making sure they don't touch each other. 6. Fry in the air fryer for 15 minutes. Make the garlic-yoghurt sauce 7. In a small bowl, combine the yoghurt, garlic, dill, and lemon juice. 8. Once the falafel is done cooking and nicely browned on all sides, remove them from the air fryer and season with salt. 9. Serve hot with a side of dipping sauce.

Buffalo Wings Honey-garlic Wings

Servings: 6
Cooking Time: 40 Minutes
Ingredients:
- FOR THE BUFFALO WINGS
- 2 pounds chicken wings
- ¼ teaspoon kosher salt
- ¼ teaspoon freshly ground black pepper
- ¼ teaspoon paprika
- 1 tablespoon vegetable oil
- ⅓ cup Buffalo wing sauce
- FOR THE HONEY-GARLIC WINGS
- 2 pounds chicken wings
- 2 tablespoons all-purpose flour
- ½ teaspoon garlic powder
- 1 tablespoon vegetable oil
- ¼ cup honey
- 2 tablespoons reduced-sodium soy sauce
- ½ teaspoon ground ginger (optional)

Directions:
1. To prep the Buffalo wings: In a large bowl, combine the wings, salt, black pepper, and paprika and toss to coat the wings with the seasonings. Drizzle with the oil.
2. To prep the honey-garlic wings: In another large bowl, combine the wings, flour, and garlic powder and toss to coat the wings. Drizzle with the oil.
3. In a small bowl, whisk together the honey, soy sauce, and ginger (if using). Set the honey-soy sauce aside.
4. To cook the wings: Install a crisper plate in each of the two baskets. Place the Buffalo wings in the Zone 1 basket and insert the basket in the unit. Place the honey-garlic wings in the Zone 2 basket and insert the basket in the unit.
5. Select Zone 1, select AIR FRY, set the temperature to 390°F, and set the time to 40 minutes. Select MATCH COOK to match Zone 2 settings to Zone 1.
6. Press START/PAUSE to begin cooking.
7. When both timers read 8 minutes, press START/PAUSE. Remove the Zone 1 basket, drizzle the Buffalo sauce over the wings, and shake to coat the wings with the sauce. Reinsert the basket. Remove the Zone 2 basket, drizzle the honey-soy sauce over the wings, and shake to coat the wings with the sauce. Reinsert the basket. Press START/PAUSE to resume cooking.
8. When cooking is complete, the wings will be golden brown and cooked through. Use silicone-tipped tongs to transfer the wings to a serving plate. Serve warm.

Nutrition:
- (Per serving) Calories: 399; Total fat: 28g; Saturated fat: 7.5g; Carbohydrates: 0g; Fiber: 0g; Protein: 34g; Sodium: 1,049mg

Fried Pickles

Servings: 4
Cooking Time: 15 Minutes
Ingredients:
- 2 cups sliced dill pickles
- 1 cup flour
- 1 tablespoon garlic powder
- 1 tablespoon Cajun spice
- ½ tablespoon cayenne pepper
- Olive Oil or cooking spray

Directions:
1. Mix together the flour and spices in a bowl.
2. Coat the sliced pickles with the flour mixture.
3. Place a crisper plate in each drawer. Put the pickles in a single layer in each drawer. Insert the drawers into the unit.
4. Select zone 1, then AIR FRY, then set the temperature to 400 degrees F/ 200 degrees C with a 15-minute timer. To match zone 2 settings to zone 1, choose MATCH. To begin, select START/STOP.

Nutrition:
- (Per serving) Calories 161 | Fat 4.1g | Sodium 975mg | Carbs 27.5g | Fiber 2.2g | Sugar 1.5g | Protein 4g

Roasted Tomato Bruschetta With Toasty Garlic Bread

Servings:4
Cooking Time: 12 Minutes
Ingredients:
- FOR THE ROASTED TOMATOES
- 10 ounces cherry tomatoes, cut in half
- 1 tablespoon balsamic vinegar
- 1 tablespoon olive oil
- ¼ teaspoon kosher salt
- ¼ teaspoon freshly ground black pepper
- FOR THE GARLIC BREAD
- 4 slices crusty Italian bread
- 1 tablespoon olive oil
- 3 garlic cloves, minced
- ¼ teaspoon Italian seasoning
- FOR THE BRUSCHETTA
- ¼ cup loosely packed fresh basil, thinly sliced
- ½ cup part-skim ricotta cheese

Directions:
1. To prep the tomatoes: In a small bowl, combine the tomatoes, vinegar, oil, salt, and black pepper.
2. To prep the garlic bread: Brush one side of each bread slice with the oil. Sprinkle with the garlic and Italian seasoning.
3. To cook the tomatoes and garlic bread: Install a broil rack in the Zone 1 basket (without the crisper plate installed). Place the tomatoes on the rack in the basket and insert the basket in the unit.
4. Place 2 slices of bread in the Zone 2 basket and insert the basket in the unit.
5. Select Zone 1, select AIR BROIL, set the temperature to 450°F, and set the time to 12 minutes.
6. Select Zone 2, select AIR FRY, set the temperature to 360°F, and set the time to 10 minutes. Select SMART FINISH.
7. Press START/PAUSE to begin cooking.
8. When the Zone 2 timer reads 5 minutes, press START/PAUSE. Remove the basket and transfer the garlic bread to a cutting board. Place the remaining 2 slices of garlic bread in the basket. Reinsert the basket in the unit and press START/PAUSE to resume cooking.
9. To assemble the bruschetta: When cooking is complete, add the basil to the tomatoes and stir to combine. Spread 2 tablespoons of ricotta onto each slice of garlic bread and top with the tomatoes. Serve warm or at room temperature.

Nutrition:
- (Per serving) Calories: 212; Total fat: 11g; Saturated fat: 2.5g; Carbohydrates: 22g; Fiber: 1.5g; Protein: 6g; Sodium: 286mg

Mexican Jalapeno Poppers

Servings: 8
Cooking Time: 5 Minutes
Ingredients:
- 5 jalapenos, cut in half & remove seeds
- ¼ tsp red pepper flakes, crushed
- 1 tsp onion powder
- 32g salsa
- 113g goat cheese
- 1 tsp garlic powder
- Pepper
- Salt

Directions:
1. In a small bowl, mix goat cheese, salsa, red pepper flakes, onion powder, garlic powder, pepper, and salt.
2. Stuff each jalapeno half with goat cheese mixture.
3. Insert a crisper plate in the Instant air fryer baskets.
4. Place stuffed peppers in both baskets.
5. Select zone 1 then select "air fry" mode and set the temperature to 360 degrees F for 8 minutes—Press "match" to match zone 2 settings to zone 1. Press "start/stop" to begin.

Crunchy Basil White Beans And Artichoke And Olive Pitta Flatbread

Servings: 6
Cooking Time: 19 Minutes
Ingredients:
- Crunchy Basil White Beans:
- 1 (425 g) can cooked white beans
- 2 tablespoons olive oil
- 1 teaspoon fresh sage, chopped
- ¼ teaspoon garlic powder
- ¼ teaspoon salt, divided
- 1 teaspoon chopped fresh basil
- Artichoke and Olive Pitta Flatbread:
- 2 wholewheat pittas
- 2 tablespoons olive oil, divided
- 2 garlic cloves, minced
- ¼ teaspoon salt
- 120 ml canned artichoke hearts, sliced
- 60 ml Kalamata olives
- 60 ml shredded Parmesan
- 60 ml crumbled feta
- Chopped fresh parsley, for garnish (optional)

Directions:
1. Make the Crunchy Basil White Beans :
2. Preheat the air fryer to 190ºC.
3. In a medium bowl, mix together the beans, olive oil, sage, garlic, ⅛ teaspoon salt, and basil.
4. Pour the white beans into the air fryer and spread them out in a single layer.
5. Bake in zone 1 basket for 10 minutes. Stir and continue cooking for an additional 5 to 9 minutes, or until they reach your preferred level of crispiness.
6. Toss with the remaining ⅛ teaspoon salt before serving.
7. Make the Artichoke and Olive Pitta Flatbread :
8. Preheat the air fryer to 190ºC.
9. Brush each pitta with 1 tablespoon olive oil, then sprinkle the minced garlic and salt over the top.
10. Distribute the artichoke hearts, olives, and cheeses evenly between the two pittas, and place both into the zone 2 air fryer basket to bake for 10 minutes.
11. Remove the pittas and cut them into 4 pieces each before serving. Sprinkle parsley over the top, if desired.

Healthy Spinach Balls

Servings: 4
Cooking Time: 15 Minutes
Ingredients:
- 1 egg
- 29g breadcrumbs
- ½ medium onion, chopped
- 225g spinach, blanched & chopped
- 1 carrot, peel & grated
- 1 tbsp cornflour
- 1 tbsp nutritional yeast
- 1 tsp garlic, minced
- ½ tsp garlic powder
- Pepper
- Salt

Directions:
1. Add spinach and remaining ingredients into the mixing bowl and mix until well combined.
2. Insert a crisper plate in the Instant air fryer baskets.
3. Make small balls from the spinach mixture and place them in both baskets.
4. Select zone 1, then select "air fry" mode and set the temperature to 390 degrees F for 10 minutes. Press "match" to match zone 2 settings to zone 1. Press "start/stop" to begin.

Sausage Balls With Cheese

Servings: 8
Cooking Time: 10 To 11 Minutes
Ingredients:
- 340 g mild sausage meat
- 355 ml baking mix
- 240 ml shredded mild Cheddar cheese
- 85 g soft white cheese, at room temperature
- 1 to 2 tablespoons olive oil

Directions:
1. Preheat the air fryer to 165ºC. Line the two air fryer baskets with parchment paper.
2. Mix together the ground sausage, baking mix, Cheddar cheese, and soft white cheese in a large bowl and stir to incorporate.
3. Divide the sausage mixture into 16 equal portions and roll them into 1-inch balls with your hands.
4. Arrange the sausage balls on the parchment, leaving space between each ball.
5. Brush the sausage balls with the olive oil. Bake in the two baskets for 10 to 11 minutes, shaking the baskets halfway through, or until the balls are firm and lightly browned on both sides.
6. Remove from the baskets to a plate.
7. Serve warm.

Fried Okra

Servings: 4
Cooking Time: 10 Minutes
Ingredients:
- 455g fresh okra
- 240ml buttermilk
- 125g plain flour
- 160g polenta
- 1 teaspoon salt
- 1 teaspoon fresh ground pepper

Directions:
1. Wash and trim the ends of the okra before slicing it into 30cm chunks.
2. In a small dish, pour the buttermilk.
3. Combine flour, polenta, salt, and pepper in a separate dish.
4. Coat all sides of okra slices in buttermilk and then in flour mixture.
5. Place a baking sheet on the baskets.
6. Press either "Zone 1" or "Zone 2" and then rotate the knob to select "Air Fryer".
7. Set the temperature to 175 degrees C, and then set the time for 5 minutes to preheat.
8. After preheating, arrange them into the basket.
9. Slide the basket into the Air Fryer and set the time for 8 minutes.
10. After cooking time is completed, place on a wire rack for a few minutes, then transfer onto serving plates and serve.

Dijon Cheese Sandwich

Servings:2
Cooking Time:10
Ingredients:
- 4 large slices sourdough, whole grain
- 4 tablespoons of Dijon mustard
- 1-1/2 cup grated sharp cheddar cheese
- 2 teaspoons green onion, chopped the green part
- 2 tablespoons of butter melted

Directions:
1. Brush the melted butter on one side of all the bread slices.
2. Then spread Dijon mustard on other sides of slices.
3. Then top the 2 bread slices with cheddar cheese and top it with green onions.
4. Cover with the remaining two slices to make two sandwiches.
5. Divide it between two baskets of the air fryer.
6. Turn on the air fry mode for zone 1 basket at 350 degrees f, for 10 minutes.
7. Use the match button for the second zone.
8. Once it's done, serve.

Nutrition:
- (Per serving) calories 617| fat 38 g| sodium 1213mg | carbs40.8 g | fiber 5g| sugar 5.6g | protein 29.5g

Crab Cake Poppers

Servings: 6
Cooking Time: 15 Minutes
Ingredients:
- 1 egg, lightly beaten
- 453g lump crab meat, drained
- 1 tsp garlic, minced
- 1 tsp lemon juice
- 1 tsp old bay seasoning
- 30g almond flour
- 1 tsp Dijon mustard
- 28g mayonnaise
- Pepper
- Salt

Directions:
1. In a bowl, mix crab meat and remaining ingredients until well combined.
2. Make small balls from the crab meat mixture and place them on a plate.
3. Place the plate in the refrigerator for 50 minutes.
4. Insert a crisper plate in the Instant air fryer baskets.
5. Place the prepared crab meatballs in both baskets.
6. Select zone 1 then select "air fry" mode and set the temperature to 360 degrees F for 10 minutes. Press "match" to match zone 2 settings to zone 1. Press "start/stop" to begin.

Bacon-wrapped Shrimp And Jalapeño

Servings: 8
Cooking Time: 26 Minutes
Ingredients:
- 24 large shrimp, peeled and deveined, about 340 g
- 5 tablespoons barbecue sauce, divided
- 12 strips bacon, cut in half
- 24 small pickled jalapeño slices

Directions:
1. Toss together the shrimp and 3 tablespoons of the barbecue sauce. Let stand for 15 minutes. Soak 24 wooden toothpicks in water for 10 minutes. Wrap 1 piece bacon around the shrimp and jalapeño slice, then secure with a toothpick.
2. Preheat the air fryer to 175°C.
3. Place the shrimp in the two air fryer baskets, spacing them ½ inch apart. Air fry for 10 minutes. Turn shrimp over with tongs and air fry for 3 minutes more, or until bacon is golden brown and shrimp are cooked through.
4. Brush with the remaining barbecue sauce and serve.

Veggie Shrimp Toast

Servings: 4
Cooking Time: 3 To 6 Minutes
Ingredients:
- 8 large raw shrimp, peeled and finely chopped
- 1 egg white
- 2 garlic cloves, minced
- 3 tablespoons minced red pepper
- 1 medium celery stalk, minced
- 2 tablespoons cornflour
- ¼ teaspoon Chinese five-spice powder
- 3 slices firm thin-sliced no-salt wholemeal bread

Directions:
1. Preheat the air fryer to 175°C.
2. In a small bowl, stir together the shrimp, egg white, garlic, red pepper, celery, cornflour, and five-spice powder. Top each slice of bread with one-third of the shrimp mixture, spreading it evenly to the edges. With a sharp knife, cut each slice of bread into 4 strips.
3. Place the shrimp toasts in the two air fryer baskets in a single layer. Air fry for 3 to 6 minutes, until crisp and golden brown.
4. Serve hot.

Cheese Corn Fritters

Servings: 6
Cooking Time: 15 Minutes
Ingredients:
- 1 egg
- 164g corn
- 2 green onions, diced
- 45g flour
- 29g breadcrumbs
- 117g cheddar cheese, shredded
- ½ tsp onion powder
- ½ tsp garlic powder
- 15g sour cream
- Pepper
- Salt

Directions:
1. In a large bowl, add all ingredients and mix until well combined.
2. Insert a crisper plate in the Instant air fryer baskets.
3. Make patties from the mixture and place them in both baskets.
4. Select zone 1, then select "air fry" mode and set the temperature to 370 degrees F for 12 minutes. Press "match" to match zone 2 settings to zone 1. Press "start/stop" to begin. Turn halfway through.

Stuffed Bell Peppers

Servings: 3
Cooking Time: 16
Ingredients:
- 6 large bell peppers
- 1-1/2 cup cooked rice
- 2 cups cheddar cheese

Directions:
1. Cut the bell peppers in half lengthwise and remove all the seeds.
2. Fill the cavity of each bell pepper with cooked rice.
3. Divide the bell peppers amongst the two zones of the air fryer basket.
4. Set the time for zone 1 for 200 degrees for 10 minutes.
5. Select MATCH button of zone 2 basket.
6. Afterward, take out the baskets and sprinkle cheese on top.
7. Set the time for zone 1 for 200 degrees for 6 minutes.
8. Select MATCH button of zone 2 basket.
9. Once it's done, serve.

Nutrition:
- (Per serving) Calories 605| Fat 26g | Sodium477 mg | Carbs68.3 g | Fiber4 g| Sugar 12.5g | Protein25.6 g

Desserts Recipes

Brownies Muffins

Servings: 3
Cooking Time: 10 Minutes
Ingredients:
- ¼ egg
- ⅛ cup walnuts, chopped
- 1 tablespoon vegetable oil
- ¼ package fudge brownie mix
- ½ teaspoon water

Directions:
1. Take a bowl, add all the ingredients. Mix well.
2. Place the mixture into prepared muffin molds evenly.
3. Line each basket of "Zone 1" and "Zone 2" with parchment paper.
4. Press "Zone 1" and "Zone 2" and then rotate the knob for each zone to select "Air Fry".
5. Set the temperature to 300 degrees F/ 150 degrees C for both zones and then set the time for 5 minutes to preheat.
6. After preheating, arrange the muffin molds into the basket of each zone.
7. Slide each basket into Air Fryer and set the time for 10 minutes.
8. After cooking time is completed, remove from Air Fryer.
9. Refrigerate.
10. Serve and enjoy!

Monkey Bread

Servings: 12
Cooking Time: 10 Minutes
Ingredients:
- Bread
- 12 Rhodes white dinner rolls
- ½ cup brown sugar
- 1 teaspoon cinnamon
- 4 tablespoons butter melted
- Glaze
- ½ cup powdered sugar
- 1-2 tablespoons milk
- ½ teaspoon vanilla

Directions:
1. Mix brown sugar, cinnamon and butter in a bowl.
2. Cut the dinner rolls in half and dip them in the sugar mixture.
3. Place these buns in a greased baking pan and pour the remaining butter on top.
4. Place the buns in the air fryer baskets.
5. Return the air fryer basket 1 to Zone 1, and basket 2 to Zone 2 of the Instant 2-Basket Air Fryer.
6. Choose the "Air Fry" mode for Zone 1 at 350 degrees F and 10 minutes of cooking time.
7. Initiate cooking by pressing the START/PAUSE BUTTON.
8. Flip the rolls once cooked halfway through.
9. Meanwhile, mix milk, vanilla and sugar in a bowl.
10. Pour the glaze over the air fried rolls.
11. Serve.

Nutrition:
- (Per serving) Calories 192 | Fat 9.3g |Sodium 133mg | Carbs 27.1g | Fiber 1.4g | Sugar 19g | Protein 3.2g

Baked Brazilian Pineapple

Servings: 4
Cooking Time: 10 Minutes
Ingredients:
- 95 g brown sugar
- 2 teaspoons ground cinnamon
- 1 small pineapple, peeled, cored, and cut into spears
- 3 tablespoons unsalted butter, melted

Directions:
1. In a small bowl, mix the brown sugar and cinnamon until thoroughly combined.
2. Brush the pineapple spears with the melted butter. Sprinkle the cinnamon-sugar over the spears, pressing lightly to ensure it adheres well.
3. Place the spears in the two air fryer drawers in a single layer. Set the air fryer to 204°C and cook for 10 minutes. Halfway through the cooking time, brush the spears with butter.
4. The pineapple spears are done when they are heated through, and the sugar is bubbling. Serve hot.

Butter Cake

Servings: 6
Cooking Time: 20 Minutes
Ingredients:
- 1 egg
- 3 tablespoons butter, softened
- ½ cup milk
- 1 tablespoon icing sugar
- ½ cup caster sugar
- 1½ cup plain flour
- A pinch of salt

Directions:
1. In a bowl, add the butter and sugar. Whisk until creamy.
2. Now, add the egg and whisk until fluffy.
3. Add the flour and salt. Mix well with the milk.
4. Place the mixture evenly into the greased cake pan.
5. Press "Zone 1" and "Zone 2" and then rotate the knob for each zone to select "Air Fry".
6. Set the temperature to 350 degrees F/ 175 degrees C for both zones and then set the time for 5 minutes to preheat.
7. After preheating, arrange the pan into the basket of each zone.
8. Slide each basket into Air Fryer and set the time for 15 minutes.
9. After cooking time is completed, remove the pan from Air Fryer.
10. Set aside to cool.
11. Serve and enjoy!

Caramelized Fruit Skewers

Servings: 4
Cooking Time: 3 To 5 Minutes
Ingredients:
- 2 peaches, peeled, pitted, and thickly sliced
- 3 plums, halved and pitted
- 3 nectarines, halved and pitted
- 1 tablespoon honey
- ½ teaspoon ground cinnamon
- ¼ teaspoon ground allspice
- Pinch cayenne pepper
- Special Equipment:
- 8 metal skewers

Directions:
1. Preheat the air fryer to 204°C.
2. Thread, alternating peaches, plums, and nectarines, onto the metal skewers that fit into the air fryer.
3. Thoroughly combine the honey, cinnamon, allspice, and cayenne in a small bowl. Brush the glaze generously over the fruit skewers.
4. Transfer the fruit skewers to the two air fryer drawers.
5. Air fry for 3 to 5 minutes, or until the fruit is caramelized.
6. Remove from the drawers.
7. Let the fruit skewers rest for 5 minutes before serving.

Butter And Chocolate Chip Cookies

Servings: 8
Cooking Time: 11 Minutes
Ingredients:
- 110 g unsalted butter, at room temperature
- 155 g powdered sweetener
- 60 g chunky peanut butter
- 1 teaspoon vanilla paste
- 1 fine almond flour
- 75 g coconut flour
- 35 g cocoa powder, unsweetened
- 1 ½ teaspoons baking powder
- ¼ teaspoon ground cinnamon
- ¼ teaspoon ginger
- 85 g unsweetened, or dark chocolate chips

Directions:
1. In a mixing dish, beat the butter and sweetener until creamy and uniform. Stir in the peanut butter and vanilla.
2. In another mixing dish, thoroughly combine the flour, cocoa powder, baking powder, cinnamon, and ginger.
3. Add the flour mixture to the peanut butter mixture; mix to combine well. Afterwards, fold in the chocolate chips. Drop by large spoonsful onto two baking paper-lined air fryer drawers. Bake at 185°C for 11 minutes or until golden brown on the top. Bon appétit!

Almond Shortbread

Servings: 8
Cooking Time: 12 Minutes
Ingredients:
- 110 g unsalted butter
- 100 g granulated sugar
- 1 teaspoon pure almond extract
- 125 g plain flour

Directions:
1. In bowl of a stand mixer fitted with the paddle attachment, beat the butter and sugar on medium speed until light and fluffy . Add the almond extract and beat until combined . Turn the mixer to low. Add the flour a little at a time and beat for about 2 minutes more until well-incorporated.
2. Pat the dough into an even layer in a baking pan. Place the pan in the zone 1 air fryer drawer. Set the air fryer to 192°C and bake for 12 minutes.
3. Carefully remove the pan from air fryer drawer. While the shortbread is still warm and soft, cut it into 8 wedges.
4. Let cool in the pan on a wire rack for 5 minutes. Remove the wedges from the pan and let cool completely on the rack before serving.

Oreo Rolls

Servings: 9
Cooking Time: 10 Minutes
Ingredients:
- 1 crescent sheet roll
- 9 Oreo cookies
- Cinnamon powder, to serve
- Powdered sugar, to serve

Directions:
1. Spread the crescent sheet roll and cut it into 9 equal squares.
2. Place one cookie at the center of each square.
3. Wrap each square around the cookies and press the ends to seal.
4. Place half of the wrapped cookies in each crisper plate.
5. Return the crisper plates to the Instant Dual Zone Air Fryer.
6. Select the Bake mode for Zone 1 and set the temperature to 360 degrees F and the time to 4-6 minutes.
7. Select the "MATCH" button to copy the settings for Zone 2.
8. Initiate cooking by pressing the START/STOP button.
9. Check for the doneness of the cookie rolls if they are golden brown, else cook 1-2 minutes more.
10. Garnish the rolls with sugar and cinnamon.
11. Serve.

Pumpkin Muffins With Cinnamon

Servings: 4
Cooking Time: 20 Minutes
Ingredients:
- 1 and ½ cups all-purpose flour
- ½ teaspoon baking soda
- ½ teaspoon baking powder
- 1 and ¼ teaspoons cinnamon, groaned
- ¼ teaspoon ground nutmeg, grated
- 2 large eggs
- Salt, pinch
- ¾ cup granulated sugar
- ½ cup dark brown sugar
- 1 and ½ cups pumpkin puree
- ¼ cup coconut milk

Directions:
1. Take 4 ramekins and layer them with muffin paper.
2. In a bowl, add the eggs, brown sugar, baking soda, baking powder, cinnamon, nutmeg, and sugar and whisk well with an electric mixer.
3. In a second bowl, mix the flour, and salt.
4. Slowly add the dry to the wet Ingredients:.
5. Fold in the pumpkin puree and milk and mix it in well.
6. Divide this batter into 4 ramekins.
7. Place two ramekins in each air fryer basket.
8. Set the time for zone 1 to 18 minutes at 360 degrees on AIR FRY mode.
9. Select the MATCH button for the zone 2 basket.
10. Check after the time is up and if not done, and let it AIR FRY for one more minute.
11. Once it is done, serve.

Honeyed, Roasted Apples With Walnuts & Rhubarb And Strawberry Crumble

Servings: 10
Cooking Time: 12 To 17 Minutes
Ingredients:
- Honeyed, Roasted Apples with Walnuts:
- 2 Granny Smith apples
- 20 g certified gluten-free rolled oats
- 2 tablespoons honey
- ½ teaspoon ground cinnamon
- 2 tablespoons chopped walnuts
- Pinch salt
- 1 tablespoon olive oil
- Rhubarb and Strawberry Crumble:
- 250 g sliced fresh strawberries
- 95 g sliced rhubarb
- 75 g granulated sugar
- 60 g quick-cooking oatmeal
- 50 g whole-wheat pastry flour, or plain flour
- 50 g packed light brown sugar
- ½ teaspoon ground cinnamon
- 3 tablespoons unsalted butter, melted

Directions:
1. Make the Honeyed, Roasted Apples with Walnuts :
2. Preheat the air fryer to 190°C.
3. Core the apples and slice them in half.
4. In a medium bowl, mix together the oats, honey, cinnamon, walnuts, salt, and olive oil.
5. Scoop a quarter of the oat mixture onto the top of each half apple.
6. Place the apples in the zone 1 air fryer basket, and roast for 12 to 15 minutes, or until the apples are fork tender.
7. Make the Rhubarb and Strawberry Crumble :
8. Preheat the air fryer to 190°C.
9. In a 6-by-2-inch round metal baking pan, combine the strawberries, rhubarb, and granulated sugar.
10. In a medium bowl, stir together the oatmeal, flour, brown sugar, and cinnamon. Stir the melted butter into this mixture until crumbly. Sprinkle the crumble mixture over the fruit.
11. Once the unit is preheated, place the pan into the zone 2 basket.
12. Bake for 12 minutes then check the crumble. If the fruit is bubbling and the topping is golden brown, it is done. If not, resume cooking.
13. When the cooking is complete, serve warm.

Baked Apples

Servings: 4
Cooking Time: 20 Minutes
Ingredients:
- 4 granny smith apples, halved and cored
- ¼ cup old-fashioned oats (not the instant kind)
- 1 tablespoon butter, melted
- 2 tablespoon brown sugar
- ½ teaspoon ground cinnamon
- Whipped cream, for topping (optional)

Directions:
1. Insert the crisper plates into the drawers. Lay the cored apple halves in a single layer into each of the drawers . Insert the drawers into the unit.
2. Select zone 1, select AIR FRY, set temperature to 350°F, and set time to 10 minutes. Select MATCH to match zone 2 settings to zone 1. Press the START/STOP button to begin cooking.
3. Meanwhile, mix the oats, melted butter, brown sugar, and cinnamon to form the topping.
4. Add the topping to the apple halves when they've cooked for 10 minutes.
5. Select zone 1, select BAKE, set temperature to 390°F, and set time to 22 minutes. Select MATCH to match zone 2 settings to zone 1. Press the START/STOP button to begin cooking.
6. Serve warm and enjoy!

Fruity Blackberry Crisp

Servings: 4
Cooking Time: 15 Minutes
Ingredients:
- 2 cups blackberries
- ⅓ cup powdered erythritol
- 2 tablespoons lemon juice
- ¼ teaspoon xanthan gum
- 1 cup Crunchy Granola

Directions:
1. Mix erythritol, blackberries, xanthan gum, and lemon juice in a large bowl.
2. Place into 6&quot| round baking dish and cover with a sheet of foil. Put into the air fryer basket.
3. Set the temperature to 350°F, then set the timer for 12 minutes.
4. When the goes off, remove the foil and shake well.
5. Sprinkle granola on the top of mixture and place back to the air fryer basket.
6. Set the temperature to 320°F, then set the timer for 3 minutes or until the top is golden brown.
7. Serve immediately.

Fried Dough With Roasted Strawberries

Servings: 4
Cooking Time: 20 Minutes
Ingredients:
- FOR THE FRIED DOUGH
- 6 ounces refrigerated pizza dough, at room temperature
- 2 tablespoons all-purpose flour, for dusting
- 4 tablespoons vegetable oil
- 2 tablespoons powdered sugar
- FOR THE ROASTED STRAWBERRIES
- 2 cups frozen whole strawberries
- 2 tablespoons granulated sugar

Directions:
1. To prep the fried dough: Divide the dough into four equal portions.
2. Dust a clean work surface with the flour. Place one dough portion on the surface and use a rolling pin to roll to a ⅛-inch thickness. Rub both sides of the dough with 1 tablespoon of oil. Repeat with remaining dough portions and oil.
3. To prep the strawberries: Place the strawberries in the Zone 2 basket. Sprinkle the granulated sugar on top.
4. To cook the fried dough and strawberries: Install a crisper plate in the Zone 1 basket. Place 2 dough portions in the basket and insert the basket in the unit. Insert the Zone 2 basket in the unit.
5. Select Zone 1, select AIR FRY, set the temperature to 400°F, and set the timer to 18 minutes.
6. Select Zone 2, select ROAST, set the temperature to 330°F, and set the timer to 20 minutes. Select SMART FINISH.
7. Press START/PAUSE to begin cooking.
8. When both timers read 8 minutes, press START/PAUSE. Remove the Zone 1 basket and transfer the fried dough to a cutting board. Place the 2 remaining dough portions in the basket, then reinsert the basket. Remove the Zone 2 basket and stir the strawberries. Reinsert the basket and press START/PAUSE to resume cooking.
9. When cooking is complete, the dough should be cooked through and the strawberries soft and jammy.
10. Sprinkle the fried dough with powdered sugar. Gently mash the strawberries with a fork. Spoon the strawberries onto each fried dough portion and serve.

Nutrition:
- (Per serving) Calories: 304; Total fat: 15g; Saturated fat: 2.5g; Carbohydrates: 38g; Fiber: 0.5g; Protein: 3g; Sodium: 421mg

Dehydrated Peaches

Servings: 4
Cooking Time: 8 Hours
Ingredients:
- 300g canned peaches

Directions:
1. Insert a crisper plate in the Instant air fryer baskets.
2. Place peaches in both baskets.
3. Select zone 1, then select "dehydrate" mode and set the temperature to 135 degrees F for 8 hours. Press "start/stop" to begin.

Nutrition:
- (Per serving) Calories 30 | Fat 0.2g | Sodium 0mg | Carbs 7g | Fiber 1.2g | Sugar 7g | Protein 0.7g

Fried Oreos

Servings: 8
Cooking Time: 8 Minutes
Ingredients:
- 1 can Pillsbury Crescent Dough (or equivalent)
- 8 Oreo cookies
- 1–2 tablespoons powdered sugar

Directions:
1. Open the crescent dough up and cut it into the right-size pieces to completely wrap each cookie.
2. Wrap each Oreo in dough. Make sure that there are no air bubbles and that the cookies are completely covered.
3. Install a crisper plate in both drawers. Place half the Oreo cookies in the zone 1 drawer and half in zone 2's. Sprinkle the tops with the powdered sugar, then insert the drawers into the unit.
4. Select zone 1, select AIR FRY, set temperature to 390°F, and set time to 8 minutes. Select MATCH to match zone 2 settings to zone 1. Press the START/STOP button to begin cooking.
5. Serve warm and enjoy!

Banana Spring Rolls With Hot Fudge Dip

Servings: 4
Cooking Time: 10 Minutes
Ingredients:
- FOR THE BANANA SPRING ROLLS
- 1 large banana
- 4 egg roll wrappers
- 4 teaspoons light brown sugar
- Nonstick cooking spray
- FOR THE HOT FUDGE DIP
- ¼ cup sweetened condensed milk
- 2 tablespoons semisweet chocolate chips
- 1 tablespoon unsweetened cocoa powder
- 1 tablespoon unsalted butter
- ⅛ teaspoon kosher salt
- ⅛ teaspoon vanilla extract

Directions:
1. To prep the banana spring rolls: Peel the banana and halve it crosswise. Cut each piece in half lengthwise, for a total of 4 pieces.
2. Place one piece of banana diagonally across an egg roll wrapper. Sprinkle with 1 teaspoon of brown sugar. Fold the edges of the egg roll wrapper over the ends of the banana, then roll to enclose the banana inside. Brush the edge of the wrapper with water and press to seal. Spritz with cooking spray. Repeat with the remaining bananas, egg roll wrappers, and brown sugar.
3. To prep the hot fudge dip: In an ovenproof ramekin or bowl, combine the condensed milk, chocolate chips, cocoa powder, butter, salt, and vanilla.
4. To cook the spring rolls and hot fudge dip: Install a crisper plate in each of the two baskets. Place the banana spring rolls seam-side down in the Zone 1 basket and insert the basket in the unit. Place the ramekin in the Zone 2 basket and insert the basket in the unit.
5. Select Zone 1, select AIR FRY, set the temperature to 390°F, and set the timer to 10 minutes.
6. Select Zone 2, select BAKE, set the temperature to 330°F, and set the timer to 8 minutes. Select SMART FINISH.
7. Press START/PAUSE to begin cooking.
8. When the Zone 2 timer reads 3 minutes, press START/PAUSE. Remove the basket and stir the hot fudge until smooth. Reinsert the basket and press START/PAUSE to resume cooking.
9. When cooking is complete, the spring rolls should be crisp.
10. Let the hot fudge cool for 2 to 3 minutes. Serve the banana spring rolls with hot fudge for dipping.

Nutrition:
- (Per serving) Calories: 268; Total fat: 10g; Saturated fat: 4g; Carbohydrates: 42g; Fiber: 2g; Protein: 5g; Sodium: 245mg

Simple Cheesecake

Servings: 3
Cooking Time: 20 Minutes
Ingredients:
- ½ egg
- 2 tablespoons sugar
- ⅛ teaspoon vanilla extract
- ¼ cup honey graham cracker crumbs
- ½ tablespoon unsalted butter, softened
- ¼ pound cream cheese, softened

Directions:
1. Line a round baking dish with parchment paper.
2. For crust: In a bowl, add the graham cracker crumbs and butter.
3. Place the crust into baking dish and press to smooth.
4. Press "Zone 1" and "Zone 2" and then rotate the knob for each zone to select "Bake".
5. Set the temperature to 350 degrees F/ 175 degrees C for both zones and then set the time for 5 minutes to preheat.
6. After preheating, arrange the baking dish into the basket of each zone.
7. Slide each basket into Air Fryer and set the time for 4 minutes.
8. Remove the crust from the oven and set aside to cool slightly.
9. Meanwhile, take a bowl, add the cream cheese and sugar. Whisk until smooth.
10. Now, place the eggs, one at a time and whisk until mixture becomes creamy.
11. Add the vanilla extract and mix well.
12. Place the cream cheese mixture evenly over the crust.
13. Arrange the baking dish into the Air-Fryer basket.
14. Remove from the oven and set aside to cool.
15. Serve and enjoy!

Biscuit Doughnuts

Servings: 8
Cooking Time: 15 Minutes
Ingredients:
- ½ cup white sugar
- 1 teaspoon cinnamon
- ½ cup powdered sugar
- 1 can pre-made biscuit dough
- Coconut oil
- Melted butter to brush biscuits

Directions:
1. Place all the biscuits on a cutting board and cut holes in the center of each biscuit using a cookie cutter.
2. Grease the crisper plate with coconut oil.
3. Place the biscuits in the two crisper plates while keeping them 1 inch apart.
4. Return the crisper plates to the Instant Dual Zone Air Fryer.
5. Choose the Air Fry mode for Zone 1 and set the temperature to 375 degrees F and the time to 15 minutes.
6. Select the "MATCH" button to copy the settings for Zone 2.
7. Initiate cooking by pressing the START/STOP button.
8. Brush all the donuts with melted butter and sprinkle cinnamon and sugar on top.
9. Air fry these donuts for one minute more.
10. Enjoy!

Moist Chocolate Espresso Muffins

Servings: 8
Cooking Time: 18 Minutes
Ingredients:
- 1 egg
- 177ml milk
- ½ tsp baking soda
- ½ tsp espresso powder
- ½ tsp baking powder
- 50g cocoa powder
- 78ml vegetable oil
- 1 tsp apple cider vinegar
- 1 tsp vanilla
- 150g brown sugar
- 150g all-purpose flour
- ½ tsp salt

Directions:
1. In a bowl, whisk egg, vinegar, oil, brown sugar, vanilla, and milk.
2. Add flour, cocoa powder, baking soda, baking powder, espresso powder, and salt and stir until well combined.
3. Pour batter into the silicone muffin moulds.
4. Insert a crisper plate in Instant air fryer baskets.
5. Place muffin moulds in both baskets.
6. Select zone 1 then select "bake" mode and set the temperature to 320 degrees F for 18 minutes. Press match cook to match zone 2 settings to zone 1. Press "start/stop" to begin.

Nutrition:
- (Per serving) Calories 222 | Fat 11g |Sodium 251mg | Carbs 29.6g | Fiber 2g | Sugar 14.5g | Protein 4g

Blueberry Pie Egg Rolls

Servings: 12
Cooking Time: 5 Minutes
Ingredients:
- 12 egg roll wrappers
- 2 cups of blueberries
- 1 tablespoon of cornstarch
- ½ cup of agave nectar
- 1 teaspoon of lemon zest
- 2 tablespoons of water
- 1 tablespoon of lemon juice
- Olive oil or butter flavored cooking spray
- Confectioner's sugar for dusting

Directions:
1. Mix blueberries with cornstarch, lemon zest, agave and water in a saucepan.
2. Cook this mixture for 5 minutes on a simmer.
3. Allow the mixture to cool.
4. Spread the roll wrappers and divide the filling at the center of the wrappers.
5. Fold the two edges and roll each wrapper.
6. Wet and seal the wrappers then place them in the air fryer basket 1.
7. Spray these rolls with cooking spray.
8. Return the air fryer basket 1 to Zone 1 of the Instant 2-Basket Air Fryer.
9. Choose the "Air Fry" mode for Zone 1 at 350 degrees F and 5 minutes of cooking time.
10. Initiate cooking by pressing the START/PAUSE BUTTON.
11. Dust the rolls with confectioner' sugar.
12. Serve.

Nutrition:
- (Per serving) Calories 258 | Fat 12.4g |Sodium 79mg | Carbs 34.3g | Fiber 1g | Sugar 17g | Protein 3.2g

Homemade Mint Pie And Strawberry Pecan Pie

Servings: 8
Cooking Time: 25 Minutes
Ingredients:
- Homemade Mint Pie:
- 1 tablespoon instant coffee
- 2 tablespoons almond butter, softened
- 2 tablespoons granulated sweetener
- 1 teaspoon dried mint
- 3 eggs, beaten
- 1 teaspoon dried spearmint
- 4 teaspoons coconut flour
- Cooking spray
- Strawberry Pecan Pie:
- 190 g whole shelled pecans
- 1 tablespoon unsalted butter, softened
- 240 ml heavy whipping cream
- 12 medium fresh strawberries, hulled
- 2 tablespoons sour cream

Directions:
1. Make the Homemade Mint Pie:
2. Spray the zone 1 air fryer drawer with cooking spray.
3. Then mix all ingredients in the mixer bowl.
4. When you get a smooth mixture, transfer it in the zone 1 air fryer drawer. Flatten it gently. Cook the pie at 185°C for 25 minutes.
5. Make the Strawberry Pecan Pie:
6. Place pecans and butter into a food processor and pulse ten times until a dough forms. Press dough into the bottom of an ungreased round nonstick baking dish.
7. Place dish into the zone 2 air fryer drawer. Adjust the temperature to 160°C and set the timer for 10 minutes. Crust will be firm and golden when done. Let cool 20 minutes.
8. In a large bowl, whisk cream until fluffy and doubled in size, about 2 minutes.
9. In a separate large bowl, mash strawberries until mostly liquid. Fold strawberries and sour cream into whipped cream.
10. Spoon mixture into cooled crust, cover, and place in refrigerator for at least 30 minutes to set. Serve chilled.

Lime Bars

Servings: 12 Bars
Cooking Time: 33 Minutes
Ingredients:
- 140 g blanched finely ground almond flour, divided
- 75 g powdered sweetener, divided
- 4 tablespoons salted butter, melted
- 120 ml fresh lime juice
- 2 large eggs, whisked

Directions:
1. In a medium bowl, mix together 110 g flour, 25 g sweetener, and butter. Press mixture into bottom of an ungreased round nonstick cake pan.
2. Place pan into the zone 1 air fryer drawer. Adjust the temperature to 148°C and bake for 13 minutes. Crust will be brown and set in the middle when done.
3. Allow to cool in pan 10 minutes.
4. In a medium bowl, combine remaining flour, remaining sweetener, lime juice, and eggs. Pour mixture over cooled crust and return to air fryer for 20 minutes. Top will be browned and firm when done.
5. Let cool completely in pan, about 30 minutes, then chill covered in the refrigerator 1 hour. Serve chilled.

Air Fryer Sweet Twists

Servings: 2
Cooking Time: 10 Minutes
Ingredients:
- 1 box store-bought puff pastry
- ½ teaspoon cinnamon
- ½ teaspoon sugar
- ½ teaspoon black sesame seeds
- Salt, pinch
- 2 tablespoons Parmesan cheese, freshly grated

Directions:
1. Place the dough on a work surface.
2. Take a small bowl and mix in cheese, sugar, salt, sesame seeds, and cinnamon.
3. Press this mixture on both sides of the dough.
4. Now, cut the pastry into 1" x 3" strips.
5. Twist each of the strips twice from each end.
6. Transfer them to both the air fryer baskets.
7. Select zone 1 to AIR FRY mode at 400 degrees F for 9-10 minutes.
8. Select the MATCH button for the zone 2 basket.
9. Once cooked, serve.

Walnuts Fritters

Servings: 6
Cooking Time: 15 Minutes.
Ingredients:
- 1 cup all-purpose flour
- ½ cup walnuts, chopped
- ¼ cup white sugar
- ¼ cup milk
- 1 egg
- 1 ½ teaspoons baking powder
- 1 pinch salt
- Cooking spray
- 2 tablespoons white sugar
- ½ teaspoon ground cinnamon
- Glaze:
- ½ cup confectioners' sugar
- 1 tablespoon milk
- ½ teaspoon caramel extract
- ¼ teaspoons ground cinnamon

Directions:
1. Layer both crisper plate with parchment paper.
2. Grease the parchment paper with cooking spray.
3. Whisk flour with milk, ¼ cup of sugar, egg, baking powder, and salt in a small bowl.
4. Separately mix 2 tablespoons of sugar with cinnamon in another bowl, toss in walnuts and mix well to coat.
5. Stir in flour mixture and mix until combined.
6. Drop the fritters mixture using a cookie scoop into the two crisper plate.
7. Return the crisper plate to the Instant Dual Zone Air Fryer.
8. Choose the Air Fry mode for Zone 1 and set the temperature to 375 degrees F and the time to 15 minutes.
9. Select the "MATCH" button to copy the settings for Zone 2.
10. Initiate cooking by pressing the START/STOP button.
11. Flip the fritters once cooked halfway through, then resume cooking.
12. Meanwhile, whisk milk, caramel extract, confectioners' sugar, and cinnamon in a bowl.
13. Transfer fritters to a wire rack and allow them to cool.
14. Drizzle with a glaze over the fritters.

Nutrition:
- (Per serving) Calories 391 | Fat 24g |Sodium 142mg | Carbs 38.5g | Fiber 3.5g | Sugar 21g | Protein 6.6g

Maple-pecan Tart With Sea Salt

Servings: 8
Cooking Time: 25 Minutes
Ingredients:
- Tart Crust:
- Vegetable oil spray
- 75 g unsalted butter, softened
- 50 g firmly packed brown sugar
- 125 g plain flour
- ¼ teaspoon kosher, or coarse sea salt
- Filling:
- 4 tablespoons unsalted butter, diced
- 95 g packed brown sugar
- 60 ml pure maple syrup
- 60 ml whole milk
- ¼ teaspoon pure vanilla extract
- 190 g finely chopped pecans
- ¼ teaspoon flaked sea salt

Directions:
1. For the crust: Line a baking pan with foil, leaving a couple of inches of overhang. Spray the foil with vegetable oil spray. 2. In a medium bowl, combine the butter and brown sugar. Beat with an electric mixer on medium-low speed until light and fluffy. Add the flour and kosher salt and beat until the ingredients are well blended. Transfer the mixture to the prepared pan. Press it evenly into the bottom of the pan. 3. Place the pan in the zone 1 air fryer drawer. Set the temperature to 176ºC and cook for 13 minutes. When the crust has 5 minutes left to cook, start the filling. 4. For the filling: In a medium saucepan, combine the butter, brown sugar, maple syrup, and milk. Bring to a simmer, stirring occasionally. When it begins simmering, cook for 1 minute. Remove from the heat and stir in the vanilla and pecans. 5. Carefully pour the filling evenly over the crust, gently spreading with a rubber spatula so the nuts and liquid are evenly distributed. Keep the air fryer at 176ºC and cook for 12 minutes, or until mixture is bubbling. 6. Remove the pan from the air fryer and sprinkle the tart with the sea salt. Cool completely on a wire rack until room temperature. 7. Transfer the pan to the refrigerator to chill. When cold, use the foil overhang to remove the tart from the pan and cut into 8 wedges. Serve at room temperature.

Easy Mini Chocolate Chip Pan Cookie

Servings: 4
Cooking Time: 7 Minutes
Ingredients:
- ½ cup blanched finely ground almond flour
- ¼ cup powdered erythritol
- 2 tablespoons unsalted butter, softened
- 1 large egg
- ½ teaspoon unflavored gelatin
- ½ teaspoon baking powder
- ½ teaspoon vanilla extract
- 2 tablespoons low-carb, sugar-free chocolate chips

Directions:
1. Combine erythritol and almond flour in a large bowl. Add in egg, gelatin, and butter, stir well.
2. Stir in vanilla and baking powder and then fold in chocolate chips. Spoon batter into 6"| round baking pan. Put pan into the air fryer basket.
3. Set the temperature to 300°F, then set the timer for 7 minutes.
4. The top of the cookie will be golden brown and a toothpick inserted in center will come out clean when fully cooked. Allow to rest for more than 10 minutes.

Cake In The Air Fryer

Servings: 2
Cooking Time: 30
Ingredients:
- 90 grams all-purpose flour
- Pinch of salt
- 1/2 teaspoon of baking powder
- ½ cup of tutti fruitti mix
- 2 eggs
- 1 teaspoon of vanilla extract
- 10 tablespoons of white sugar

Directions:
1. Take a bowl and add all-purpose flour, salt, and baking powder.
2. Stir it in a large bowl.
3. Whisk two eggs in a separate bowl and add vanilla extract, sugar and blend it with a hand beater.
4. Now combine wet ingredients with the dry ones.
5. Mix it well and pour it between two round pan that fits inside baskets.
6. Place the pans in both the baskets.
7. Now set the zone 1 basket to BAKE function at 310 for 30 minutes.
8. Select MATCH for zone two baskets.
9. Once it's done, serve and enjoy.

Nutrition:
- (Per serving) Calories 711| Fat4.8g| Sodium 143mg | Carbs 161g | Fiber 1.3g | Sugar 105g | Protein 10.2g

Molten Chocolate Almond Cakes

Servings: 3
Cooking Time: 13 Minutes
Ingredients:
- Butter and flour for the ramekins
- 110 g bittersweet chocolate, chopped
- 110 gunsalted butter
- 2 eggs
- 2 egg yolks
- 50 g granulated sugar
- ½ teaspoon pure vanilla extract, or almond extract
- 1 tablespoon plain flour
- 3 tablespoons ground almonds
- 8 to 12 semisweet chocolate discs (or 4 chunks of chocolate)
- Cocoa powder or icing sugar, for dusting
- Toasted almonds, coarsely chopped

Directions:
1. Butter and flour three ramekins.
2. Melt the chocolate and butter together, either in the microwave or in a double boiler. In a separate bowl, beat the eggs, egg yolks and sugar together until light and smooth. Add the vanilla extract. Whisk the chocolate mixture into the egg mixture. Stir in the flour and ground almonds.
3. Preheat the air fryer to 165°C.
4. Transfer the batter carefully to the buttered ramekins, filling halfway. Place two or three chocolate discs in the center of the batter and then fill the ramekins to ½-inch below the top with the remaining batter. Place the ramekins into the zone 1 air fryer basket and air fry for 13 minutes. The sides of the cake should be set, but the centers should be slightly soft. Remove the ramekins from the air fryer and let the cakes sit for 5 minutes.
5. Run a butter knife around the edge of the ramekins and invert the cakes onto a plate. Lift the ramekin off the plate slowly and carefully so that the cake doesn't break. Dust with cocoa powder or icing sugar and serve with a scoop of ice cream and some coarsely chopped toasted almonds.

Apple Fritters

Servings: 14
Cooking Time: 10 Minutes

Ingredients:
- 2 large apples
- 2 cups all-purpose flour
- ½ cup granulated sugar
- 1 tablespoon baking powder
- 1 teaspoon salt
- 1 teaspoon ground cinnamon
- ½ teaspoon ground nutmeg
- ¼ teaspoon ground cloves
- ¾ cup apple cider or apple juice
- 2 eggs
- 3 tablespoons butter, melted
- 1 teaspoon vanilla extract
- For the apple cider glaze:
- 2 cups powdered sugar
- ¼ cup apple cider or apple juice
- ½ teaspoon ground cinnamon
- ¼ teaspoon ground nutmeg

Directions:

1. Peel and core the apples, then cut them into ¼-inch cubes. Spread the apple chunks out on a kitchen towel to absorb any excess moisture.
2. In a mixing bowl, combine the flour, sugar, baking powder, salt, and spices.
3. Add the apple chunks and combine well.
4. Whisk together the apple cider, eggs, melted butter, and vanilla in a small bowl.
5. Combine the wet and dry in a large mixing bowl.
6. Install a crisper plate in both drawers. Use an ice cream scoop to scoop 3 to 4 dollops of fritter dough into the zone 1 drawer and 3 to 4 dollops into the zone 2 drawer. Insert the drawers into the unit. You may need to cook in batches.
7. Select zone 1, select BAKE, set temperature to 390°F, and set time to 10 minutes. Select MATCH to match zone 2 settings to zone 1. Press the START/STOP button to begin cooking.
8. Meanwhile, make the glaze: Whisk the powdered sugar, apple cider, and spices together until smooth.
9. When the fritters are cooked, drizzle the glaze over them. Let sit for 10 minutes until the glaze sets.

Spiced Apple Cake

Servings: 6
Cooking Time: 30 Minutes

Ingredients:
- Vegetable oil
- 2 diced & peeled Gala apples
- 1 tablespoon fresh lemon juice
- 55 g unsalted butter, softened
- 65 g granulated sugar
- 2 large eggs
- 155 g plain flour
- 1½ teaspoons baking powder
- 1 tablespoon apple pie spice
- ½ teaspoon ground ginger
- ¼ teaspoon ground cardamom
- ¼ teaspoon ground nutmeg
- ½ teaspoon kosher, or coarse sea salt
- 60 ml whole milk
- Icing sugar, for dusting

Directions:

1. Grease a 0.7-liter Bundt, or tube pan with oil; set aside.
2. In a medium bowl, toss the apples with the lemon juice until well coated; set aside.
3. In a large bowl, combine the butter and sugar. Beat with an electric hand mixer on medium speed until the sugar has dissolved. Add the eggs and beat until fluffy. Add the flour, baking powder, apple pie spice, ginger, cardamom, nutmeg, salt, and milk. Mix until the batter is thick but pourable.
4. Pour the batter into the prepared pan. Top batter evenly with the apple mixture. Place the pan in the zone 1 air fryer drawer. Set the temperature to 176°C and cook for 30 minutes, or until a toothpick inserted in the center of the cake comes out clean. Close the air fryer and let the cake rest for 10 minutes. Turn the cake out onto a wire rack and cool completely.
5. Right before serving, dust the cake with icing sugar.

RECIPES INDEX

A

Acorn Squash Slices 32

Air Fried Bacon And Eggs 15

Air Fried Chicken Potatoes With Sun-dried Tomato 63

Air Fried Lamb Chops 72

Air Fried Sausage 28

Air Fryer Meatloaves 76

Air Fryer Sweet Twists 95

Almond Shortbread 90

Apple Fritters 98

arlic-herb Fried Squash 34

Asian Pork Skewers 80

Asparagus And Bell Pepper Strata And Greek Bagels 15

B

Bacon Cheese Egg With Avocado And Potato Nuggets 16

Bacon Wrapped Corn Cob 35

Bacon Wrapped Pork Tenderloin 80

Bacon, Cheese, And Avocado Melt & Cheesy Scrambled Eggs 22

Bacon-and-eggs Avocado And Simple Scotch Eggs 20

Bacon-wrapped Chicken 64

Bacon-wrapped Filet Mignon 70

Bacon-wrapped Shrimp And Jalapeño 87

Bagels 17

Baked Apples 91

Baked Brazilian Pineapple 88

Baked Peach Oatmeal 24

Balsamic Duck Breast 65

Balsamic Vegetables 34

Banana Spring Rolls With Hot Fudge Dip 93

Bang Bang Shrimp With Roasted Bok Choy 43

Basil Cheese S·saltalmon 50

Bbq Cheddar-stuffed Chicken Breasts 58

Bbq Pork Spare Ribs 71

Beef And Bean Taquitos With Mexican Rice 75

Beef Skewers 81

Bell Pepper Stuffed Chicken Roll-ups 65

Biscuit Doughnuts 94

Blue Cheese Steak Salad 77

Blueberry Pie Egg Rolls 94

Breakfast Potatoes 26

Breakfast Sausage And Cauliflower 26

Brownies Muffins 88

Buffalo Bites 31

Buffalo Chicken 55

Buffalo Chicken Breakfast Muffins 25

Buffalo Seitan With Crispy Zucchini Noodles 36

Buffalo Wings Honey-garlic Wings 83

Butter And Chocolate Chip Cookies 89

Butter Cake 89

Buttered Mahi-mahi 38

Buttermilk Biscuits With Roasted Stone Fruit Compote 24

Buttermilk Fried Chicken 54

C

Cajun Breakfast Sausage 27

Cajun Catfish Cakes With Cheese 50

Cajun Scallops 43

Cake In The Air Fryer 97

Canadian Bacon Muffin Sandwiches And All-in-one Toast 29

Caprese Panini With Zucchini Chips 35

Caramelized Fruit Skewers 89

Cheddar-ham-corn Muffins 29

Cheddar-stuffed Chicken 56

Cheese Corn Fritters 87

Cheese Drops 82

Cheesy Scrambled Eggs And Egg And Bacon Muffins 23

Chicken & Veggies 57

Chicken And Broccoli 63

Chicken And Potatoes 67

Chicken And Vegetable Fajitas 61

Chicken Caprese 66

Chicken Leg Piece 60

Chicken Legs With Leeks 66

Chicken Tenders 82

Chicken With Pineapple And Peach 59

Chili Honey Salmon 39

Chili Lime Tilapia 42

Chipotle Drumsticks 67

Cilantro Lime Steak 80

Classic Fish Sticks With Tartar Sauce 48

Cod With Jalapeño 42

Codfish With Herb Vinaigrette 53

Cornish Hen With Asparagus 66

Cornish Hen With Baked Potatoes 55

Crab Cake Poppers 86

Crispy Fried Quail 62

Crispy Sesame Chicken 54

Crunchy Basil White Beans And Artichoke And Olive Pitta Flatbread 85

Crusted Chicken Breast 59

Curried Orange Honey Chicken 57

Curry-crusted Lamb Chops With Baked Brown Sugar Acorn Squash 73

D

Dehydrated Peaches 92

Dijon Cheese Sandwich 86

E

Easy Breaded Pork Chops 81

Easy Mini Chocolate Chip Pan Cookie 97

Egg And Bacon Muffins 22

Egg White Muffins 20

Eggs In Avocado Cups 29

F

Fajita Chicken Strips & Barbecued Chicken With Creamy Coleslaw 56

Falafel 38

Fish And Chips 41

Fish Tacos 44

Five-ingredient Falafel With Garlic-yoghurt Sauce 83

Flavorful Salmon Fillets 45

Fried Artichoke Hearts 34

Fried Asparagus 32

Fried Avocado Tacos 30

Fried Dough With Roasted Strawberries 92

Fried Lobster Tails 47

Fried Okra 86

Fried Oreos 92

Fried Pickles 84

Fried Prawns 46

Fruity Blackberry Crisp 91

Furikake Salmon 52

G

Garlic Bread 81

Garlic Butter Prawns Scampi & Coconut Prawns 49

Garlic Butter Steaks 76

Garlic Shrimp With Pasta Alfredo 47

Garlic-rosemary Pork Loin With Scalloped Potatoes And Cauliflower 79

GGarlic-rosemary Brussels Sprouts 33

Glazed Thighs With French Fries 65

Goat Cheese-stuffed Bavette Steak 71

Goat Cheese–stuffed Chicken Breast With Broiled Zucchini And Cherry Tomatoes 61

Gochujang Brisket 78

Green Beans With Baked Potatoes 37

Green Salad With Crispy Fried Goat Cheese And Baked Croutons 33

H

Hawaiian Chicken Bites 69

Healthy Spinach Balls 85

Herb Lemon Mussels 53

Homemade Mint Pie And Strawberry Pecan Pie 95

Honey-baked Pork Loin 77

Honeyed, Roasted Apples With Walnuts & Rhubarb And Strawberry Crumble 91

Honey-glazed Chicken Thighs 62

Hot Dogs Wrapped In Bacon 76

I

Italian Baked Cod 42

J

Jalapeño Popper Egg Cups And Cheddar Soufflés 21

Jerk Chicken Thighs 59

Juicy Duck Breast 58

K

Kale And Spinach Chips 31

Kale Chips 82

L

Lemon Butter Salmon 40

Lemon Chicken Thighs 57

Lemon-pepper Trout 49

Lime Bars 95

M

Maple-pecan Tart With Sea Salt 96

Marinated Ginger Garlic Salmon 42

Mexican Jalapeno Poppers 84

Minute Steak Roll-ups 70

Moist Chocolate Espresso Muffins 94

Mojito Lamb Chops 75

Molten Chocolate Almond Cakes 97

Monkey Bread 88

Mushroom-and-tomato Stuffed Hash Browns 16

Mustard Pork Chops 73

Mustard Rubbed Lamb Chops 79

N

Nutty Granola 27

O

Onion Omelette And Buffalo Egg Cups 18

Oreo Rolls 90

P

Parmesan Fish Fillets 51

Parmesan Mackerel With Coriander And Garlic Butter Prawns Scampi 45

Parmesan Sausage Egg Muffins 28

Perfect Cinnamon Toast 26

Pigs In A Blanket With Spinach-artichoke Stuffed Mushrooms 74

Potato And Parsnip Latkes With Baked Apples 37

Potatoes & Beans 36

Potatoes Lyonnaise 17

Prawn Dejonghe Skewers 46

Pretzel-crusted Catfish 40

Pumpkin Muffins With Cinnamon 90

R

Ranch Turkey Tenders With Roasted Vegetable Salad 60

Red Pepper And Feta Frittata 22

Red Pepper And Feta Frittata And Bacon Eggs On The Go 14

Roasted Beef 78

Roasted Garlic Chicken Pizza With Cauliflower "wings" 64

Roasted Salmon Fillets & Chilli Lime Prawns 52

Roasted Tomato Bruschetta With Toasty Garlic Bread 84

Rosemary Asparagus & Potatoes 31

S

Salmon Quiche 23

Sausage & Bacon Omelet 17

Sausage And Egg Breakfast Burrito 27

Sausage Balls With Cheese 85

Sausage Meatballs 70

Sausage With Eggs 25

Sausage-stuffed Peppers 72

Scallops 46

Scallops And Spinach With Cream Sauce And Confetti Salmon Burgers 51

Sesame Bagels 25

Simple Bagels 14

Simple Beef Sirloin Roast 73

Simple Cheesecake 93

Simple Strip Steak 78

Simply Terrific Turkey Meatballs 55

Smoked Salmon 50

Snapper Scampi 52

Spiced Apple Cake 98

Spicy Chicken 68

Spicy Chicken Sandwiches With "fried" Pickles 69

Spinach Omelet And Bacon, Egg, And Cheese Roll Ups 21

Steak And Asparagus Bundles 74

Steamed Cod With Garlic And Swiss Chard 45

Stuffed Beef Fillet With Feta Cheese 77

Stuffed Bell Peppers 87

Stuffed Sweet Potatoes 32

Sumptuous Pizza Tortilla Rolls 72

Sweet Potato Sausage Hash 18

T

Tandoori Prawns 40

Tasty Lamb Patties 71

Tender Juicy Honey Glazed Salmon 39

Teriyaki Chicken Skewers 58

Thai Chicken With Cucumber And Chili Salad 68

Tilapia Sandwiches With Tartar Sauce 44

Tomato And Mozzarella Bruschetta And Portobello Eggs Benedict 28

Tuna Patties 48

Tuna Patties With Spicy Sriracha Sauce Coconut Prawns 39

Tuna With Herbs 53

Turkey Ham Muffins 19

Two-way Salmon 49

V

Vanilla Strawberry Doughnuts 19

Veggie Shrimp Toast 87

W

Walnuts Fritters 96

Wholemeal Blueberry Muffins 19

Wild Rice And Kale Stuffed Chicken Thighs 67

Y

Yummy Chicken Breasts 62

Z

Zucchini With Stuffing 30

Printed in Great Britain
by Amazon